T0193116

MODERN-DAY

Holy Woman

A 40-DAY BIBLE STUDY

JESSICA ROTHMEYER PHD

WESTBOW
PRESS®
A DIVISION OF THOMAS NELSON
& ZONDERVAN

WestBow Press books may be ordered through booksellers or by contacting:

WestBow Press
A Division of Thomas Nelson & Zondervan
1663 Liberty Drive
Bloomington, IN 47403
www.westbowpress.com
844-714-3454

ISBN: 978-1-6642-3288-4 (sc)
ISBN: 978-1-6642-3287-7 (hc)
ISBN: 978-1-6642-3289-1 (e)

Library of Congress Control Number: 2021908763

Print information available on the last page.

WestBow Press rev. date: 06/18/2021

Jessica Rothmeyer
www.kindgom-mindset.org

CONTENTS

INTRODUCTION

Welcome to *Modern-Day Holy Woman,* a Bible study on 1 Peter 3. After counseling women individually and co-facilitating biblical marriage counseling for over 20 years, I have a great deal of passion to teach the Godly wisdom found in these particular verses. In these pages, we will look at how to live out your biblical role in marriage as a wife, who you are to represent as a woman in the community, and who you are called to be as a Christ-follower. This is an eight-week study, each week containing five days of teaching, reflection, and journaling, giving us a total of 40 days. In these 40 days, I pray you will receive great revelation from God about the powerful truth found in this chapter of Scripture.

To support the mindset Peter is trying to establish in this chapter, I will also draw on many other Scripture quotes from other books of the Bible. God's Word is beautifully fluid—a magnificent tapestry of His love and truth that is consistent from the Old to the New Testament, book to book, chapter to chapter, and verse to verse. Learning to study God's Word increases your wisdom and your trust in who God says He is, as well as who *you are* to Him. As you study the Bible and begin to see God's promises *never change,* you will realize His Word is timeless: perfectly applicable to the lives of men and women in biblical times, yet also offering vital direction and truth for our lives today.

Each day will end with a reflection section, which is very important. Do not skip this section; it will cause the information you read each day to be woven into the fabric of your soul. Application is essential for permanent change. If you read this book individually, you can simply self-reflect and journal your answers. But I strongly suggest reading it with a group, using the reflection questions for discussion, and sharing personal struggles and testimonies. This provides an opportunity to learn from and to encourage one another.

Almost nothing has brought me more joy, as a Christian counselor and a spiritual mentor, than teaching women the *powerful* position and *holy* calling that God has predestined for each one of His precious daughters. So, join me on this spiritually challenging and life-changing study, and discover your significant role in God's Kingdom as a *modern-day holy woman*.

WEEK ONE

Winning People for Christ

In the same way, you wives, be subject to your own husbands so that even if any of them are disobedient to the word, they may be won without a word by the behavior of their wives, as they observe your pure and respectful behavior (1 Peter 3:1–2 NASB).

This week we will learn how to be pure and respectful in the face of adversity. Sometimes people (including your husband) may not treat you as wonderfully as you treat them. Or at least, they may not treat you how you think they *should* treat you. But learning to react in Christ-like ways, even in difficult situations, is a very important Kingdom principle. As we pursue being *holy* and having a God-honoring lifestyle, we must train ourselves to react in ways that are not instinctual and may even seem weird. At times, your response might even be labeled as unhealthy by the spiritually ignorant. In order to truly encapsulate the role of a modern-day holy woman, you must retrain your mind and heart to align with God's heart and mind, no longer agreeing with the world you live in. In these first two verses of 1 Peter 3, we are called as wives to win our husbands for Christ by our pure and respectful behavior. This is a challenge, yet also a great honor.

DAY ONE

A Godly Response

*In the same way, you wives, be subject to your own husbands so **that even if any of them are disobedient to the word**, they may be won without a word by the behavior of their wives, as they observe your pure and respectful behavior* (1 Peter 3:1–2 NASB).

I love that the NASB translation labels this section of Scripture as *Godly Living*. Different translations vary slightly in titling certain chapters. This is because the Bible's original text was not divided into verses and chapters, and it did not include heading titles. These were added later to help the reader study and comprehend God's truth in a clear way. Other translations usually label this chapter as special instructions to *Husbands and Wives*. But, as we are going to study *all* of chapter 3, not just verses 1–7, I appreciate this version's title: *Godly Living*.

As important as the first few words are, for now we are going to lightly pass over the topic of being subject, or submissive, as we will address it in more depth during week three. For this week's study, we are going to embrace the idea of how women are to *win* their husbands (and all people) over through our pure (pure of heart, sanctified by God) and respectful behavior, even when it is most difficult.

Since my education is in psychology, I often integrate the scientific theories and schools of thought I learned at university into how I give spiritual counsel. So, let's talk a little modern brain science. This verse suggests that as a woman, mother, and wife you are to have pleasant and quiet (peaceable) responses, even when others are acting poorly toward you (being disobedient to the Word). Reacting this way is very *anti-instinctual*.

Humans (both men and women) have an automatic response when being offended, which is often called *acting defensive,* but it is also the brain's natural response of self-preservation. All humans want to defend and preserve the (God-given) idea that they are valuable, worthy, and good in nature. Therefore, when accused, most people will respond with anger, frustration, explanations, or passive expressions such as sighing, eye-rolling, or grunting. Others will not react, but try to swallow or stuff their feelings for the benefit of the relationship or to avoid conflict. That often leads to headaches, stomachaches, depression, and anxiety. What is the correct response? The secular world has no good answers for this.

The only truth that lasts in this life is found in the mindset and behaviors of Christ and the desire to live out *that kind* of holiness and righteousness. *"But like the Holy One who called you, be holy yourselves also in all your behavior; because it is written: 'You shall be Holy, for I am holy'"* (1 Pet. 1:15–16 NASB).

The definition of *holy* is: "to be devoted entirely to God and His work and to seek complete devotion to the One who is perfect in goodness and righteousness." With this kind of heart and affection toward your Father in Heaven, based on the example set by Jesus, you are to demonstrate what it looks like to win people (especially your husband) for Christ without saying a word.

How many times did Jesus win people over with His *conduct* rather than His words? Often people made harsh and untrue accusations about Him, or acted hatefully toward Him, yet Jesus remained calm and responded respectfully with love. But in everyday life, reacting and responding like Jesus can be very, very difficult. This is especially true when the harsh words and unloving actions toward you come from those you love the most and who *should* love you in return.

But if you are able to have a kind response, or perhaps none at all, with a pure heart, viewing the offensive behaviors of others through a forgiving, Christ-like perspective, it will lessen your instinctual reaction over time. Eventually, you will simply respond from the overflow of God's love for you, coming through you and onto others. It is God's greatest desire that each and every one of His children would come into full alignment with the attributes He placed in you, so as to win as many souls as possible for the Kingdom. Your efforts will be rewarded both in your life now and in heavenly rewards. Not only that, but this is the *only way* to sustain a healthy soul and protect yourself from undue suffering, both in your body and in the spiritual realm.

Reflection

- Journal about a time or two when you have been offended by your husband or a situation that seems to happen over and over in your marriage that really hurts your feelings.
- What kinds of words, accusations, or unkind actions leave you thinking, "How could he?"
- After reading this section, how can you resist your natural reaction to self-preserve the next time unkind words or actions come your way and instead respond with Christ-like love?
- How could you change your mindset in preparation for such times, so as to prepare your heart and mind to react in a peaceable way and avoid becoming resentful or unforgiving later?

_____

_____

_____

_____

_____

_____

_____

_____

_____

_____

_____

_____

_____

_____

_____

DAY TWO

Being Falsely Accused

*In the same way, you wives, **be subject to your own husbands so that even if any of them are disobedient to the word, they may be won without a word by the behavior of their wives**, as they observe your pure and respectful behavior* (1 Peter 3:1–2 NASB).

The command to remain quiet and gentle when your husband (or others you love) are disobedient to the Word could apply to a variety of scenarios. For today's example, let's consider being falsely accused. Remaining silent or responding in kindness in this situation goes against every human instinct. Refusing to become defensive or give a rebuttal, even when you know the other person is wrong and you are feeling attacked, is so hard. Many marital conflicts occur when spouses make accusations toward one another, usually in a moment of trying to be heard or in an attempt to have their emotional needs met. Instead of meeting these needs, it turns the conversation into a defensive battle that leaves both parties wounded. What kind of behavior and response did Jesus have in similar situations?

> *And while He was being accused by the chief priests and elders, He did not offer any answer. Then Pilate said to Him, "Do You not hear how many things they are testifying against You?" And still He did not answer him in regard to even a single charge, so the governor was greatly amazed* (Matthew 27:12–14 NASB).

It is frustrating when someone accuses you of saying, thinking, or feeling something you actually did not say, think, or feel. Even more infuriating is when people accuse you of *being* someone or something you are not, hitting you at the core of your identity. How upsetting it is when others do not recognize or validate who you *really* are.

Psychologically, I think being accused of something you did not do or say is one of the most helpless feelings. Often when this happens, an inner battle occurs in an attempt to rationalize what was said or reconcile the assault on one's identity, which can cause anger, anxiety, ruminating thoughts, and a whole list of physical issues such as headaches, digestive issues, and skin rashes.

Jesus experienced being falsely accused often in His time of ministry, but never so fiercely as when He was being tried for a crime He did not commit, knowing He would die for it (for us).

I try to remember this on days when I am particularly frustrated, when I am feeling misunderstood, or when I am wishing for more validation from my husband, family, or friends. *Why don't they see who I really am? Haven't I demonstrated my good-will and love to them hundreds of times? Why do they only seem to point out the worst in me?* In these moments, the most important question is: How will I respond to their false accusations? Do I respond without a word, like Jesus did, like 1 Peter 3:2 is instructing? Unfortunately, many Jews and the High Priests were *not* won over in the moment when Jesus stayed silent. But did they question themselves when the world went black and the temple walls shook as Jesus died on the cross? Were they, perhaps, among the thousands who were converted on Pentecost, realizing what they had done and recognizing Jesus *as* the Son of the living God?

As I studied Scripture through a lens of trying to help people heal, one Kingdom principle became clear: There will be times when we do not completely understand the outcome of our circumstances or receive the perfect answer to our prayers in our desired timing. But we can *trust* in the example Jesus set for us during His time here on earth—showing that one who lives a holy and righteous lifestyle is blessed. I have had a few successes in showing grace and resisting becoming defensive in the midst of accusation, and I was very aware of how pleasing my obedience was to the Lord. I have witnessed this behavior have *powerful results* in my marriage, and it has hugely benefited my mental and emotional health. Scripture says even Pilate was greatly amazed when Jesus stayed silent, because he assumed all the things the religious leaders were saying about Jesus were not true. We must never underestimate the impact of our example on those we interact with on a daily basis. Is it your heart's desire to be Christ-like in all that you say and do, both to obey and to be an example?

Reflection

- Journal about a time when you were able to successfully stay quiet in the midst of being falsely accused, not receiving justification, or feeling unheard.
- What happened? How did you feel?
- Did you receive confirmation or validation from God about how pleasing this behavior was to Him? (Because it *always* is.)
- Do you have a testimony of how your consistent Christ-like behavior had an impact on your marriage and family?

Jessica Rothmeyer PhD

DAY THREE

Rejection

In the same way, you wives, be subject to your own husbands **so that even if any of them are disobedient to the word, they may be won without a word by the behavior of their wives,** *as they observe your pure and respectful behavior* (1 Peter 3:1–2 NASB).

Rejection by Family and Friends

It would be nice to think that if we as wives, mothers, sisters, and daughters would simply apply the truth in these verses, we could quickly or instantly transform our families, but that is not necessarily the case. Often, we must be very persistent, as it can perhaps take years or even a lifetime before we see any true change. At times, a woman will make great efforts to be Godly in her interactions, yet she is rejected rather than appreciated. This is the very thing that keeps many people in self-protection mode, leading to resentment and bitterness. Rejection is a significant reason why people suffer from mental and emotional health issues. Learning to adopt the mind and heart of Christ is our best chance in living a victorious, hope-filled life. So, let's take a look at a few scenarios in Jesus' life that are similar to what we might experience in our marriages, families, and the community:

> *And they took offense at Him. But Jesus said to them, "A prophet is not dishonored except in his hometown and in his own household." And He did not do many miracles there because of their unbelief"* (Matthew 13:57–58 NASB).

This was how Jesus was treated in His hometown of Nazareth. No one wanted to believe He was anything special, because they had known Him as a child, and they definitely did not believe He was the Messiah. Jesus says a prophet often does not receive honor in his or her own hometown or family. I have counseled many women who have been dishonored by their husband, children, or friends because of their bold faith. Isn't it comforting to know that Jesus suffered in the same way? If His own people did not believe *Him* or treat *Him* with honor, who are we to be upset when we face the same treatment?

Rejection by Community or Church

Although today's verse is specifically speaking to how a wife is to win her *husband* over, this spiritual truth can be applied more broadly to how women act within their community and church family. Let us look to Jesus' example in how we are to react if we are treated poorly or rejected by those from whom we seek validation, inclusion, and acceptance:

> *When the days were approaching for His ascension, He was determined to go to Jerusalem; and He sent messengers on ahead of Him, and they went and entered a village of the Samaritans to make arrangements for Him. And they did not receive Him, because He was traveling toward Jerusalem. When His disciples James and John saw this, they said, "Lord, do You want us to command fire to come down from heaven and consume them?" But He turned and rebuked them, [and said, "You do not know what kind of spirit you are of; for the Son of Man did not come to destroy men's lives, but to save them."] And they went on to another village* (Luke 9:51–56 NASB).

I think one cannot help but cheer a little inside for the way in which the disciples reacted after they came back with the news that the Samaritans would not receive Jesus. Samaritans and Jews were not always on the same page spiritually, but this was Jesus. Surely they had heard of the wonderful miracles He had performed. Some had even personally experienced His kindness (see John 4). But Jesus' response was not to give them an earful; rather, He moved on to another town and rebuked His students for wanting revenge. He reminded them that, as Christ-followers, we are here to save lives, not destroy them. We are here to bless and not curse. We are called to respond in the Kingdom way—with love, not in the same way we were treated. This is challenging, but righteous. I promise you, it will bring the highest level of peace and healing to your life.

Reflection

- Journal about a specific way you have felt dishonored or rejected by your loved ones because of your faith.
- Journal about a time or two when you have felt angered by how you were treated by a community or church and wished *you* could "pray down fire" from Heaven. What did you say, or how did you react? How did you get past those feelings, or do you continue to struggle with hurt feelings today?
- What could be your mindset going forward in regard to rejection? Looking to the example of Jesus, could you accept being rejected for His sake and for the greater good of God's Kingdom?

DAY FOUR

Responding in Love

In the same way, you wives, be subject to your own husbands so that even if any of them are disobedient to the word, they may be won without a word by the behavior of their wives, as they observe your pure and respectful behavior (1 Peter 3:1–2 NASB).

Early on in my professional counseling career, I experienced a great deal of resistance in trying to address the above biblical truths—particularly with the business-oriented, independent, and success-driven women of the 2000s. (I began my counseling career in May of 2000.) As with our faith, our desire to be holy and righteous in the way the Bible teaches needs to come from a deep relationship with Christ. If you have not surrendered your life to Christ and declared Him to be your Lord and Savior, this study may not inspire you, and you will most definitely lose the perseverance needed to live out these challenges in the long run. (See Appendix 1 at the end of this book for a salvation prayer. If you believe it in your heart and declare it aloud, you will be saved, and you will then open the gateway to having an intimate relationship with God.)

If you are already a Christ follower, you will find joy, healing, and freedom in your desire to be refined into the likeness of Christ, with the powerful help of the Holy Spirit, through the deeper understanding and application of this study. I say all of that to bring you to the most significant truth in these first two verses: It is *hard* to have pure and respectful behavior with a husband who is *not obeying* the Word of God. In order to be successful in living out these words, you must have a deep yearning to be Christ-like by the power of the Holy Spirit. Otherwise, you assuredly will become discouraged and then discontinue your efforts. Or even worse, you will become resentful and bitter toward your husband's (children's, friend's, family's) lack of change in response to your white-knuckle efforts to "kill them with kindness."

But responding with love, grace, and mercy while being treated less kindly than you deserve is very Godly. This is a specific command given to women by God in order to call us into our *full power and influence* in the lives of our husbands, children, and the greater community. Because women are created to be relationship experts and nurturers and have the ability to display gentle mercy in life's circumstances (all examples given to us by Christ), your demonstration of these characteristics is an impactful expression of holiness and righteousness to those around you. Whether they acknowledge your efforts or not, God *sees* it all, and your efforts through personal sacrifice are *very important* to Him.

Reflection

- Journal about a time or two, or about an overarching theme in your life, when in your heart of hearts you *wanted* to be kind and loving, no matter how others treated you, and yet, when they failed to notice your efforts or reciprocate, you were left feeling hopeless, angry, or resentful. What did you do? How long did it last?
- What is your motivation for being submissive, pure, and respectful?
- Should that motivation be different, based on today's study?

DAY FIVE

Being Ignored, Dismissed, or Betrayed

*In the same way, you wives, be subject to your own husbands so that **even if any of them are disobedient to the word, they may be won without a word by the behavior of their wives, as they observe your pure and respectful behavior*** (1 Peter 3:1–2 NASB).

Ignored or Dismissed

In all my years of marriage counseling, this is the most common complaint that causes a wife great pain: being ignored and dismissed by her husband and children. Why do we have to act like crazy people before they will listen to us? Or perhaps you are the type to swallow your feelings, but then you wonder why you have unidentified anxiety or often feel depressed? It is part of our God-given design, as women, to want approval. We long to be loved for *who we are,* not for how we act or what we might say during an emotional time of stress or chaos.

In the following passage of Scripture, Jesus is in the garden of Gethsemane, preparing to be arrested and crucified. He had asked three of His trusted disciples to come with Him to pray. But they almost immediately fell asleep. *"And He came to the disciples and found them sleeping, and He said to Peter, 'So, you men could not keep watch with Me for one hour?'"* (Matt. 26:40). Here, Jesus did say *something*, but not as much as He could have. How frustrating it must have been for Him when His faithful friends fell asleep three times, leaving Him alone in His time of fear and turmoil when they had promised to pray for Him.

How often have you felt this way? When you most need emotional support, you are vulnerable and cry out, only to have your loved one leave you. They ignore or dismiss you to deal with it on your own, because they are too tired or do not want to deal with your difficult emotions. Be comforted. Jesus had this same experience. He tried to urge the disciples to stay awake, to keep watch, to prayerfully intercede for Him. But they did not stay awake for even *one hour*. And yet Jesus died for those men.

Sometimes, when I am feeling hurt, dismissed, and ignored by my loved ones, meditating on Jesus' real-life scenarios, like this one, humbles me. Jesus deserved so much love, honor, and respect, and yet He too was ignored and dismissed. How alone and desperately sad was Jesus in the garden—asking His Father twice if this cup could pass from Him, praying so fervently that He sweat blood? Many holy women throughout history have passionately cried out to the Lord with great emotion and grief in their times of distress. If this is, or has been, you at one time or another, Jesus *knows* how you feel; when your loved ones let you down, when you are alone in your pain, or when you express your need for help, and it seems like no one is listening— Jesus sees you. He has compassion for you, and He is listening.

Betrayed

The most heartbreaking stories I have heard as a marriage counselor are those of betrayal. To betray, deceive, or deny the one person you are called to love more than any other cuts a heart so deeply that even the most faith-filled believers struggle to recover. Jesus also knows this pain, as we see in the following Scripture:

> *But Peter replied to Him, "Even if they all fall away because of You, I will never fall away!" Jesus said to him, "Truly I say to you that this very night, before a rooster crows, you will deny Me three times"* (Matthew 26:33–34 NASB).

Here is Peter, the disciple who loved Jesus with such a passion that He was always first to defend and protect Him. Peter walked on water in faith (even though he had a minor lapse in focus and began to sink); he was the only one to get out of the boat! And finally, Peter was the first to boldly declare that Jesus was the Christ, the Son of the living God (see Matt. 16:16). When Jesus said that every one of the disciples would fall away when He was arrested, that they would all deny Him, Peter tried to assure Jesus that he would be willing to die with Him and would never betray Him. But we all know how that story ends. Peter did indeed deny Jesus three times, and Jesus was left alone in His suffering, knowing He was betrayed by those who claimed to love Him most.

Like Peter, most of us have good intentions in the beginning of a relationship—until the heat is on and the pressure cooker of life begins to test our spiritual strength. Will we react like Jesus and forgive the betrayal, learning to love again and repeatedly sacrifice for the *very person* who abandoned us in our time of need? Jesus did it for Peter. After Jesus rose from the dead, in order to restore grace and reignite their intimate connection, Jesus asked Peter three times if He loved Him (see John 21:15–17). He asked one time for every time Peter had denied Him. How beautiful is that? These questions were for Peter's sake, not for Jesus' sake.

It is kind of ironic that it was Peter who asked Jesus how many times he must forgive others. This indicates he was having trouble forgiving and wanted to know when enough was enough. Jesus responded with abundant grace and said the standard was not the seven times Peter suggested, but seventy times seven. However many times *we think* someone should be forgiven or feel like someone has hurt us one too many times, if we reflect on the words and truth found in the Bible and look to the example of Jesus, we see that we are called to forgive again, to love again. And further, we are called to win them over for Christ with our love, the love of Christ. We must be ever-vigilant in our words and actions; the world (and our spouse, kids, friends, extended family, and community) is watching.

As D. L. Moody once said, "Out of 100 men, one will read the Bible, the other 99 will read the Christian."[1]

---

[1] D.L. Moody Quotes, *D.L. Moody*, www.sermonindex.net.

Reflection

- Journal about a time when you felt dismissed or an area in which you feel alone and ignored by your loved ones.
- How do you typically respond?
- Have you found anything that helps? Assertive communication? Prayer? Or do you have a lot of resentments in this area?
- How could the life examples of Jesus soften your heart and bring you peace?
- We pledge to love one another in sickness and in health at the marriage altar, but how often will a husband be patient and understanding to his wife when she is in a bad mood?
- Will a husband comfort his wife even when he thinks her emotions are silly? Will he be faithful even when his needs are not being met?
- And will you, as a wife, love your husband by showing him grace and respect, even when he is not meeting your needs or expectations?
- Journal about a time when you felt betrayed by your spouse. Or, (if your spouse has expressed it to you) how have they felt *betrayed by you*?
- How do you and your spouse reconcile after a time of feeling betrayed or abandoned?
- Are you able to forgive and truly let go, even if there is *no* resolution to the conflict and no validation for your feelings about it?

Jessica Rothmeyer PhD

WEEK TWO

Godly Beauty

Your adornment must not be merely the external—braiding the hair, wearing gold jewelry, or putting on apparel; but it should be the hidden person of the heart, with the imperishable quality of a gentle and quiet spirit, which is precious in the sight of God (1 Peter 3:3–4 NASB).

Teaching on Godly beauty has become a very poignant and healing subject in the last ten years of my career. The wisdom and truth found in these verses is timeless. As our culture continues down a path of worldly desires and biblical ignorance, both women (and men) need to learn *how to live* in an atmosphere that is inundated with daily messages of perfectionism, eternal youth, and false realities. We are taught to find joy in our outward appearance—whether through clothing, dying our hair, false nails and eyelashes, professional cosmetics, diets, workout routines, or plastic surgery. Whole societies and social demographics that would have otherwise not been very concerned with outward appearance are now, due to the internet, obsessed with the elusive fountain of youth and seeking "followers" on social platforms. Common people are hoping they will become the next internet superstar and influencer simply by posting a filtered picture or a self-promoting video. How do I see this social and interpersonal phenomenon from a mental, emotional, and spiritual health perspective? People have never been as unhealthy or discontent as in these modern times. So, let us discover how God would instruct us to think, feel, and behave in this area of our lives.

DAY ONE

Idolatry

Your adornment must not be merely the external—braiding the hair, wearing gold jewelry, or putting on apparel; but it should be the hidden person of the heart, with the imperishable quality of a gentle and quiet spirit, which is precious in the sight of God (1 Peter 3:3–4 NASB).

Early on in my counseling career, God highlighted a Kingdom message to me that is woven throughout Scripture: God cares about the *heart*. The sooner a person realizes this, the healthier they are mentally, emotionally, and spiritually. These two verses, 1 Peter 3:3–4, are a reminder to women in particular that it is in our nature to enjoy looking beautiful, but what really matters in life is seeking God above all else. In return, He cares about our inner being, the heart, *above all else*.

The world does not talk about idolatry much anymore. For most of human history, different belief systems and religions have worshiped idols. Idol worship often included food offerings, wearing necklaces, bowing to statutes, and even human sacrifices. In modern times, some people make their job, a sport they like to play, or even their marriage an idol. Many would say a movie star, a famous singer, or a significant person in history is their idol. Never before has the world emphasized the need for a person to be beautiful, youthful, thin, and perfect as much as it does in our modern times, thus making *ourselves* the idol. The majority of the ads we view on television and social media every day are about exercise programs, weight-loss schemes, and professional cosmetics.

Perhaps you are thinking, "I just want to look nice. Why shouldn't I spend a little money on myself? It helps with my self-esteem. Beauty isn't an *idol* in my life." But most people do not comprehend all that this word really means or the spiritual *power* idols have to cause pain and suffering in their overall well-being. After witnessing the destructive effects idols produce in the lives of my clients, family, and friends over the years, *hidden idols* is a topic I teach on with passion and urgency. The first commandment given in the Old Testament is: *"You shall have no other gods* [idols] *before Me"* (Exod. 20:3 NASB).

Surely, you might say, "I do not have any other *gods* before God." But the enemy is sneaky, and it is his greatest pleasure to deceive us into allowing the things of this world to infiltrate our hearts and take priority or precedence over a fervent, laser-focused relationship with Jesus. After all, Satan was thrown down from Heaven because of *his* idolatress heart. He was jealous of God and wanted to be considered a god. He knows very well how this type of sinful thinking and alignment with evil will lead to separation from God. By contrast, Jesus emphasizes: *"You shall love the Lord your God with all your heart, and with all your soul, and with all your strength, and with all your mind… "* (Luke 10:27 NASB).

In other words, you should love God with *all that you are*. Seek to love the Lord your God with your full attention. Even then, you will never come close to loving Him as much as He loves you. I am praying that through this study each reader will come to a greater understanding of the spiritual power in these words: Love God *above all else*. Your mental and emotional health depend on it. The effectiveness of your prayers and the level of influence your testimony has on others will be determined by the degree to which you protect your heart. Don't let any god, idol, or worldly longing take the place reserved for the one true God.

Reflection

- What is an idol(s) in your life? Your kids? Your career? Your ministry? Wanting to be thin and beautiful? Remember, an idol could be any hinderance or distraction in your life that would keep you from loving God with your whole mind, heart, and soul.
- Do you recognize how you first began to align your thinking and eventually your heart's desires with something that initially appeared innocent, but then led to great pain or discontentment in your life?
- In times when you have had victory over an idol in your heart, what were the results in your life of making God first?

_____

_____

_____

_____

_____

_____

_____

_____

_____

_____

_____

_____

_____

_____

_____

_____

DAY TWO

Modern Challenges

Your adornment must not be merely the external—braiding the hair, wearing gold jewelry, or putting on apparel; but it should be the hidden person of the heart, with the imperishable quality of a gentle and quiet spirit, which is precious in the sight of God (1 Peter:3-4 NASB).

Several years ago, when I first began teaching on the topic of Godly beauty, I reflected on what life must have been like for the holy women of the past. During biblical times, most women would have been covered with clothing from head to toe. As this week's verses suggest, the way in which women of old *concerned themselves* with their outward appearance was to simply braid their hair or wear gold jewelry. What would the holy women *of old* think of beauty today? What would they think of indoor tanning, teeth whitening, plastic surgery, false eyelashes, dyed hair, acrylic nails, diet pills and shakes, and obsessive exercising? What would they think of women posting scantily dressed pictures of themselves on social media to get the "likes" that make them feel special? Because of modern technology, fantasy beauty and pornography are easily available to every man, woman, and child. I doubt the holy women of biblical times would have believed that our world's current level of ungodliness could be possible. The biblical meaning of beauty is a very different reality from what is portrayed and coveted today. I believe the obsession with beauty, glamour, and fame is one of the biggest spiritual challenges of modern society, which is warring against a Godly and righteous lifestyle based in humility.

Maybe you feel a little defensive and wonder, "Does that mean I should just let myself go and not care about how I look so I can be considered a *holy woman?*" The answer is *no*. But there is a very thin line between taking care of yourself physically—maybe wearing a little make-up, fixing your hair nicely, and wearing new clothes—and spending a huge percentage of your time, energy, and income on your appearance. I have done a great deal of research in this area for the purposes of this study, and I've found that the amount of money women (and men) spend on cosmetics and items related to their outward appearance could feed the starving children of the world twice over. I am not trying to make you feel bad or ashamed. This is a very difficult and sensitive subject. I give you this truth with the greatest of care for your mental and spiritual health. I have been teaching about Godly beauty for over two decades, and *I am still tempted* to be caught up in the world's alluring promises of being thin, beautiful, and forever youthful.

Not only is this idolatry, but it steals a great deal of time and money from our purpose of advancing the Kingdom of God. Think of all the money you could invest in supporting your local church, donating to community outreach, or building a well for fresh water in a village in a third world country. The pursuit of worldly beauty also steals people's joy, because it is a lie. Any happiness your outward appearance might bring you is fleeting. At the end of the day, your make up comes off, your hair turns grey, your skin sags, and your clothes are no longer in season.

Does this mean it is sinful to go to the hairdresser to cover up those greys? Or is God going to be disappointed in you if you buy mascara that costs more than ten dollars? The answer is not purely in how much time or money those things cost you *in the natural*, but rather in how much they cost you in your relationship with Jesus. The Bible says, *"Those who pay regard to vain idols forsake their hope of steadfast love"* (Jonah 2:8 ESV). This may be a short verse, but it is full of wisdom about the human struggle against idolatry and a loss of love. A steadfast love heals and grounds people like *nothing* in this world can.

If you aren't rooted in God's unconditional love for you and engaged in an on-going pursuit to stay in the presence of His love, you will be drawn to rely on the love or comfort of *anything* of this world, and it will inevitably lead to a very unhealthy lifestyle. In my experience, women who focus on their outward appearance or their abilities, performance, and achievements will fall prey to jealousy and competition and will struggle with their own self-esteem. These women also tend to be more inwardly focused and self-concerned. Christ has called *all believers* to serve in humility, choosing to sacrifice and focus on serving others before themselves.

As I have counseled teenagers over the course of twenty years, I have watched the growing popularity of social media and self-promotion have devastating effects on our youth. Sadly, it is not contained to the teen population any longer. Adults of all ages and genders are suffering from depression, anxiety, FOMO (fear of missing out), FOBAN (fear of being a nobody), and a whole host of related physical issues (which we will cover in the next section) that arise from viewing themselves through the lens of the world. The world's lens is false; it is edited and filtered. We are grieving a reality that does not exist. Worldly perfectionism and youthful beauty are lies from the enemy that try to pervert the promise and truth of the authentic eternity that God has in store for believers in Heaven. Eternal youth is not for us here on this earth; it is an evil illusion designed to steal our joy, make us competitive and jealous of one another, and eventually make us despise or reject ourselves as we age. No wonder Satan spends so much of his time and effort deceiving the world into believing outward beauty needs to be such a priority. Look at the destruction he has accomplished through it!

Focusing on one's outward appearance can be as destructive to your mental, emotional, and spiritual health as any type of childhood abuse or life trauma. I have seen many women try to have good self-esteem or feel happy by losing weight, buying new clothes, or achieving some kind of challenging goal. Although it might bring some joy in the moment, that kind of happiness is temporary and will eventually leave them feeling discontent, wanting more, and envying others.

The *only* true joy we can rely on—the joy that girds us up, grounds us, and gives us our true worth, value, and purpose—is the joy of discovering the steadfast, relentless, and never-ending love of God.

Reflection

- In what ways do you struggle to love your outward appearance?
- Have you been able to resist jealousy or not be envious of others who are smarter, prettier, thinner, or more noticed by the world than you?
- Were your efforts successful? How long did it last before you felt discouraged again?
- Do you struggle with self-hatred or self-rejection? (By the way, we *all* do to some degree.) In which ways, specifically? What do you think God would want you to believe about who you are and who *He* created you to be? (Find Scripture verses to support your answers.)
- Have you had an experience when the love of the Father was so all-encompassing and overwhelming in your life that things like beauty, your weight, and worldly accomplishments seemed so small in the grand scheme of God's Kingdom? When have you viewed your life from the perspective of eternity (will it matter in Heaven)?
- Meditate for a moment about how much more valuable your appearance in Heaven will be, when you receive your glorified body, which will be more than you could ever hope for or imagine here on this earth?

DAY THREE

Guard Your Heart

Your adornment must not be merely the external—braiding the hair, wearing gold jewelry, or putting on apparel; **but it should be the hidden person of the heart,** *with the imperishable quality of a gentle and quiet spirit, which is precious in the sight of God* (1 Peter 3:3–4 NASB).

For the majority of my counseling career, I engaged in consistent Bible study and conducted research that would lead me, my clients, my family, and my friends into deeper healing for the mind, soul, and *body*. From a very young age, I had God-given faith to believe in supernatural miracles. I wanted to first understand and then teach these spiritual truths to others in order to release God's healing in their lives. Through my observations while working with people day in and day out, I realized that there are spiritual, emotional, and mental roots to most physical diseases in the body. God gave me case study after case study in which I saw people supernaturally healed by addressing the *spiritual* root to their *physical* problems. The Bible affirms this reality:

> *So above all, guard the affections of your heart, for they affect all that you are. Pay attention to the welfare of your innermost being, for from there flows the wellspring of life* (Proverbs 4:23 TPT).

I used the Passion Translation for this verse because it best explains what I saw in my counseling office every day. Some translations say, *"for from it, come all issues in life."* If you have not considered this area of your faith, or the effects of the spiritual realm in your physical life before, let me assure you that this Kingdom principle *is real.* Many experts in the science and medical fields, even those who would make no specific claim to faith, admit that many physical issues are basically *caused* by mental and emotional (and I would add spiritual) problems.

In my research and real-life case studies, I've found that some of the most common physical issues caused by idolatry of one's outward appearance are skin rashes, eczema, warts, acne, bloated stomach, inability to lose weight (even when you diet), eating disorders, inflammatory related-diseases, and chronic pain issues, especially arthritis. This is not an exhaustive list, but I think it proves that if we allow *anything* other than the love of God to fulfill us, validate our worth, or be the driving force for who we are in life, *we will suffer.* Many women would admit that being overweight or not liking a particular physical feature gravely affects their happiness level and can be quite consuming in their daily thinking, thereby affecting their mood and overall emotional health. But how often do we reflect on the damage this idolatry is doing to our physical bodies?

As I taught my clients about how the idols of their hearts (and the wounds of their souls) affect their physical bodies, I witnessed many supernatural miracles. One woman was completely healed of arthritis, another healed of eczema, and many, many women were set free from life-long eating disorders and weight-loss issues. The most common factors I found present in my clients who struggled to lose weight (especially those women who would exercise and eat clean and still did not see the scale move) were feelings of self-rejection, self-hatred, unworthiness, and being not good enough. Until this mental, emotional, and spiritual wound is healed, it is unlikely such people will be able to lose weight and keep it off. Nor will they find freedom to fully grasp their value and worth *spiritually,* independent from their physical looks.

When people release their desire for worldly beauty, thinness, perfection, recognition from others, and obsession with self, and instead choose to seek the ever-abiding love of God, we get a beautiful glimpse of Kingdom living. Great freedom and life-changing healing *always* takes place at the feet of Jesus! But this healing journey will take on-going effort. The world and its prince, Satan, will try to tempt you back into bondage through a constant news feed of perfectionism and cosmetic fixes, to superficially soothe your soul or give you false hope. But as you pursue *guarding your heart* from these vanities and truly seek God with all that you are, you will experience mental, emotional, and physical healing, and you will actually *appear* more beautiful. Only through repeatedly rejecting the false teachings and priorities of this world and becoming solely devoted to Almighty God can you achieve your best life.

Scripture is clear, through the prophet Isaiah, that Jesus was nothing extraordinary to look at. It was solely the glory and love of God shining through Him that caused people to become enamored by His appearance and long to be in His presence. *"…He has no stately form or majestic splendor that we would look at Him, nor [handsome] appearance that we would be attracted to Him"* (Isa. 53:2 AMP).

As Jesus-followers, we are all called to be glory-carriers, to mesmerize and drastically impact the non-believers of this world—not by our worldly beauty, but by God's beauty in us. As you spend time in God's presence and guard your heart, supernatural healing *will happen*, and you will manifest His love and glory through your *physical body*! Luke describes something like this happening to Jesus on the mount of transfiguration: *"As He was praying, the appearance of His face became different [actually transformed], and His clothing became white and flashing with the brilliance of lightning"* (Luke 9:29 AMP).

I can attest to this transformation personally and in the lives of many of my clients; as they healed their minds and hearts and learned to stay in God's abiding love, they *actually appeared* more beautiful in the natural. The opposite is true as well. We can probably all think of people who are naturally very beautiful, but when we encounter their ugly heart, their appearance dramatically changes, and suddenly we do not think they are as pretty as they once were. The heart is where Godly beauty lies. From that place, you will be transformed, over and over, until your final transformation in eternity.

Reflection

- Spend some time reflecting and then journaling about your feelings relating to worldly beauty.
- What kinds of physical ailments do you suffer from that perhaps could be related to the idols or wounds in your heart relating to your outward appearance?
- Have you ever experienced supernatural healing after realizing and then releasing such an idol?

DAY FOUR

The Missing Component

Your adornment must not be merely the external—braiding the hair, wearing gold jewelry, or putting on apparel; but it should be the hidden person of the heart, with the imperishable quality of a gentle and quiet spirit, which is precious in the sight of God (1 Peter 3:3–4 NASB).

One component of life that has radically changed since biblical times is how women interact with one another. I believe competition and division has happened among females due to the percentage of women working outside the home, the rise of social media, and the worldly focus on *self-promotion*. If we reflect on how women related to one another throughout most of history, we will realize that they spent a great deal of time together. They helped each other do chores; they would often cook together and wash clothes together; and they would help each other prepare for special ceremonies. They also served as nurse for each other, using mostly love, prayers, and homemade remedies when family members fell ill. They would also aid in teaching and mentoring each other's children. Women were there for each other, helping to support one another emotionally and spiritually as they spent many hours a day together.

I heard a story once about a missionary group who constructed a fresh-water well in a small village in the Middle East. But the locals kept destroying it with explosives. Three times the missionaries rebuilt the well before they discovered that the village *wives* were destroying the well. Although it was more than a mile walk, one way, to retrieve water, the women wanted to continue their tradition, because it gave them valuable time each day to talk and emotionally support one another, since many of these women were in abusive or oppressive relationships. Water collection was necessary for daily life; therefore, it was approved by their husbands. This chore provided the village women with *life-sustaining* time with one another as a supportive group.

In our society, it is difficult to find women who are part of a close-knit group. Perhaps you are doing this Bible study right now with some of your friends or through a church group, and I applaud you. Such groups are growing rare. How often do women need to cancel plans with girlfriends or go weeks in between get-togethers because of their busy, task-filled lives? How many women have few or no other close female relationships? We have become a very isolated and technology-driven society. God created humans for relationship—*first with Him* and then with each other. A supportive tribe of female friends, prayer warriors, and faith-filled armor-bearers is something *every* woman needs in order to thrive mentally, emotionally, and spiritually.

I know for a fact, as a mental health professional, that the drastic increase in depression and anxiety diagnoses in the last ten years is largely due to isolation and trying to survive on fake technology-based friendships through social media. The fact is, a person can be on their phone 24/7, liking posts, watching videos, and even texting constantly, but this is *not* the same as being face to face with someone and interacting with another *person*. Having times of vulnerability and intimacy with others is very healing to the human soul. This is the type of environment in which God created every man, woman, and child to thrive in, not one that isolates you and leaves you feeling alone, unnoticed, and unsupported.

In order for future generations to recover from a very unhealthy downward spiral culturally, we must teach, coach, and model the value of being women who *seek each other out*. We must lift each other up, serve one another, make efforts to leave the comfortable or apathetic place on our couch, and seek out *real and authentic* relationships with other women. How quickly we would see jealousy, competition, and comparison die if we would allow ourselves to enter into deep relationship with other women.

I am warning you: It will not be easy. Satan knows the powerful influence and authority of a group of strong Christian women connected in truth and love. These groups of women are unstoppable, so he will try to throw distraction, busy schedules, and demanding jobs in your path. But with wisdom and Spirit-led conviction, the modern-day holy woman will return to her biblical roots and be exactly who God called her to be—loving, caring, and supportive of others, particularly other women. The collective influence of women who band together is exponential. Every woman could experience significant increase in health and stability by borrowing faith from her fellow females; by offering support to one another financially, medically, and emotionally; by helping to raise and teach each other's children; and by supporting each other when walking through difficult life circumstances. The impact women can have on this earth will be explosive if we persevere in our efforts to connect and be of one accord!

Reflection

- Do you have a group, tribe, or friendship circle of women you can rely on? What are some of the obstacles you have encountered in pursuing strong, faith-filled, intimate relationships with other women?
- How might you view yourself, other women, and even your relationship with God when surrounded by other healthy, supportive women?
- Share an experience of victory or healing due to the prayers and support of other women in your life.

DAY FIVE

Imperishable Beauty

*Your adornment must not be merely the external—braiding the hair, wearing gold jewelry, or putting on apparel; but it should be the hidden person of the heart, **with the imperishable quality of a gentle and quiet spirit, which is precious in the sight of God*** (1 Peter 3:3–4 NASB).

This is the kind of beauty that never dies. With all the modern science, professional make-up, and plastic surgery in the world today, many women are on the hunt for the ever-elusive fountain of youth. Most people cannot afford these types of elite beauty interventions, but many women continue to long for this glamorous lifestyle. I have witnessed many women chasing this dream by spending more time, money, and effort toward being thin, young-looking, and physically healthy than they do toward any other goal in their lives.

I had a young female client who was a Christian, was newly married, and had every possible gift and ability to be a happy and successful woman, but she was miserable. She was depressed, anxious, and had many resentments concerning past female friendships in her life. She was very focused on her health and became a fitness guru and practiced cosmetology, so she always had the newest hairstyles and perfect make-up. Yet where was her joy? She claimed to have good self-esteem, and she worked hard to look as good as she did, but she continued to feel discontent. The pivotal moment in her counseling experience was when I challenged her to read her Bible for as many minutes a day as she would train at the gym. I also challenged her to tithe to her church or give monetary donations to those in need each month in the same amount as she would spend on her cosmetics, hair products, and clothing. It was a challenge she accepted with anxious tears—but it changed her life.

I am focusing on this idea of how modern women are overly concerned with their outward appearance because I have seen the pure destruction it causes in women's lives. But I also want to balance this admonishment with Godly affirmation: You can dye your hair, buy a new outfit, and wear make-up *as long as you keep God first* in your heart and do not let your outward appearance affect whether you feel loved, diminish your worth, or cause you to compare yourself to others. And exercise is of course good and important. We are a very sedentary society compared to women throughout history; they would have performed manual labor all day long while completing their daily tasks. They had to walk many miles every day for simple things like food and water. And if you think laundry is bad now, imagine having to bang your clothes against a rock! So exercise is good, but be careful not to let your exercise be for vain efforts, or you will allow a foothold for Satan. He will whisper lies of never-ending longings and self-focused desires to you, which will lead to mental, emotional, and spiritual bondage. If our bodies are to be the temple of the Holy Spirit (see 1 Cor. 6:18–19), then we must take care of our bodies for *that reason*, not to be noticed by others or to feel good about ourselves. I can assure you, from counseling thousands of women, that beauty and outward appearance are *not* where joy, self-worth, or contentment reside.

I truly do not know of another spiritual or emotional bondage that causes as much mental, emotional, spiritual, and physical oppression and disease in women as an ungodly desire for outward beauty. The modern woman feels unloved, unnoticed, rejected, alone, and unworthy *because at some point* she received a message from the world that she was not beautiful, and the vicious cycle of self-hatred and the hatred of other women began. So, what is the answer? Let's see what God says about this issue:

> But the LORD said to Samuel, "Do not look at his appearance or at the height of his stature, because I have rejected him; for God does not see as man sees, since man looks at the outward appearance, but the LORD looks at the heart" (1 Samuel 16:7 NASB).

It is my greatest passion to teach people how to view their lives and themselves through a Kingdom perspective, through the eyes of Christ. God does not see us the way the world sees us. In order to be healthy of mind, heart, and body and to remain strong in the daily spiritual battles in our lives (while we remain on this earth), it is *essential* to learn to think like God thinks about every area of our lives. We must constantly view our thoughts and feelings through a Kingdom filter in order to survive and thrive. I believe this skill is needed more than ever, because our world is so far off the mark from living and teaching a God-honoring lifestyle. We can no longer trust the instructions of this world, even if they sound good. We must always test it against the only absolute truth there is, which is found in the Word of God.

> *All Scripture is God-breathed [given by divine inspiration] and is profitable for instruction, for conviction [of sin], for correction [of error and restoration to obedience], for training in righteousness [learning to live in conformity to God's will, both publicly and privately—behaving honorably with personal integrity and moral courage]; so that the man of God may be complete and proficient, outfitted and thoroughly equipped for every good work* (2 Timothy 3:16–17 AMP).

In our verse of the week, the Holy Spirit teaches us that it is the *"hidden person of the heart"* that is so pleasing and precious to God. Jesus teaches in depth on this Kingdom principle in Matthew 6. He presents a completely different mindset than that of the religious leaders and scholars at the time. Jesus said (paraphrased), when you pray, go into a closet and do it in secret. When you give of your time, talent, or money, do it when no one is watching so that you do not give yourself any credit. And when you fast, tell no one and look and act like you are not suffering at all so no one would guess that you are fasting.

Jesus is teaching a crucial Kingdom principle that leads to mental and emotional vitality and spiritual strength. But these concepts are very different from the self-promoting emphasis on beauty, being noticed, and validation-from-others lifestyle promoted by our modern world. God looks at the *hidden* person of the heart. This is Godly thinking: Give in secret, pray in secret, fast in secret, serve and sacrifice for others without the validation you think you *deserve*, and your reward will be great. Perhaps it will be a reward of wealth, success, physical health, prosperity in your family, a thriving marriage, or a fruitful ministry. Sometimes you will not reap your *full* reward until you go to Heaven, but it will be worth it, and it will be extravagant!

Joyce Meyer once said that she knew she was already receiving a lot of her reward here on this earth for her ministry efforts. She would give this advice to up-and-coming authors, public speakers, and preachers experiencing some degree of fame: "Hear that applause? See all those messages of gratitude in your email or on your social media posts? Hope you enjoy it, because that is all the glory you are going to get for it."[2] But what about those who serve, sacrifice, and do good in secret? The home-school mom, the custodian at church, the nursing home aide, the one serving a meal to the homeless—*these people* will have a far greater reward in Heaven, because God sees their self-less acts. Being humble and giving in secret are precious and holy in His eyes.

As I have walked *many people* through these lessons and watched as they accepted them as biblical truth, I have seen their lives transformed. People were healed mentally, emotionally, and physically. They became firmly planted in their faith by applying a Kingdom mindset to their circumstances. And most importantly, the intensity of their love for the Father grew. When you experience the revelation of how much He loves you, how He created you for a reason and a purpose, and that He wants you to know that you are noticed, worthy, and loved (and it has *nothing* to do with your outward appearance)—that is the space where miraculous healing happens. You will never be the same afterward, mind, body, or spirit.

Reflection

- Can you think of a time (or times) when you have been led astray by the teachings of this world about your outward appearance and it has left you feeling sad, resentful, or hopeless?

---

[2] Enjoying Everyday Life TV Show, *Joyce Meyer Ministries*, www.joycemeyer.org.

- How have you challenged your thoughts and feelings with what God has to say about you and your situation instead of being focused on vanity?
- Do you think you would approach your life issues differently knowing what Scripture has to say about Godly beauty?
- Journal and discuss with other women about times when you have submitted without saying a word, sacrificed when you were already tired or weak, served when no one served you, and suffered quietly for the greater good—and you *believed God saw you*, the hidden person of the heart. Did you know He was pleased? Did you realize these behaviors were considered imperishable beauty, which is all that really matters in the end?
- Did you know these are great acts of obedience that will cause spiritual change in you? Did you know that God will use these selfless acts of kindness and your desire to be gentle and peaceable *above* being justified or heard, to make you holier and more like Him? How does *that* make you feel?

WEEK THREE

Holy Women of Old

For in this way the holy women of former times, who hoped in God, also used to adorn themselves, being subject to their own husbands, just as Sarah obeyed Abraham, calling him lord; and you have proved to be her children if you do what is right without being frightened by any fear (1 Peter 3:5–6 NASB).

As we look at verses five and six this week, we will focus on who the holy women of old were, how they thought and behaved, what their culture was like at the time, and how their culture affected how they operated as the daughters of Sarah in God's Kingdom. In order to be a modern-day holy woman, one must first understand what this role looked like in the biblical context and then apply those traits and characteristics to our modern situations. I have been teaching women for years how to think and act in Godly ways, but our current times call for a warrior spirit to rise up in every believer, more than ever before, in order to abandon the worldly teachings of today and return to the truth that brings healing and victory to our lives.

DAY ONE

Trust and Hope in the Lord

For in this way the holy women of former times, who hoped in God, also used to adorn themselves, being subject to their own husbands, just as Sarah obeyed Abraham, calling him lord; and you have proved to be her children if you do what is right without being frightened by any fear (1 Peter 3:5–6 NASB).

"The holy women...who hoped in God...." This is how they adorned themselves—they put their trust and hope in the Lord, not in their husbands, not in modern science, not in a medical professional, not in a self-help book. They adorned themselves with hope in God. The 1828 edition of *Merriam-Webster's Dictionary* defines *adorn* this way: "to make more pleasing, to display the beauty or excellence of the doctrine of God."[3] Holy women were and are considered beautiful as they adorn themselves by putting their hope in God's promises from His Word. True beauty comes from trusting Him to provide, protect, and complete all they would ever need.

Whether you were betrayed by your father, abused by a man as a child or teen, or you have experienced infidelity, abuse, or neglect from your husband, learning to put your hope and trust in the Lord, *more than* relying on a man to meet or fulfill your needs, is a crucial step in becoming a modern-day holy woman. This biblical truth is not just true in regard to

---

[3] *Webster's Dictionary:Unabridged,* by Noah Webster, 1828.

our fathers and husbands, but to all humankind. Afterall, the Word refers to people as fools or foolish over 60 times throughout Scripture. I am sure we can all think of a time, maybe even today, when someone we thought loved us decided to treat us poorly, betray us, or make us feel unloved. Only Father God can be trusted to never leave us, always providing His supernatural love and protection in our lives.

> *Do not trust in princes, in mortal man, in whom there is no salvation (help).... How blessed and graciously favored is he whose help is the God of Jacob (Israel), whose hope is in the* Lord *his God* (Psalm 146:3,5 AMP).

I counseled many women who have said, "I have trust issues." Sadly, not being able to trust others leads to many mental health and emotional issues. And withholding your trust, being unforgiving, or trying to stay in self-protection mode will not lead you into healthy relationships. So, as faith-filled believers, we must choose to put our *full* hope and trust in the Lord, knowing He will be there for us *no matter what* the humans in our lives say or do. As you nurture an intimate relationship with the Holy Spirit, He will guide you in who to trust (as much as you can in a human) or not trust based on the person and situation.

Learning to let go of unhealthy expectations for your husband, children, and friends is an excellent way to stay emotionally healthy and strong of mind. It is one of the first areas of discussion when I mentor a young woman—learning to see her husband through God's eyes, coming to realize he is not her god or her everything, and discovering that *her role* should be more of a concern and priority in her daily life than criticizing what her husband is or isn't doing to please her. Every believer, man or woman, should not put their health and well-being in the hands of others, but put their full faith and trust in the Promise-maker. Learning to put your hope and trust in God does not mean you stop looking to your spouse for love and affection, though. God created him to be a very special counterpart in the greater picture of what marriage symbolizes. (We will discuss this topic further next week.) But a woman's peace of mind and emotional well-being *cannot* be tied to her husband; this unhealthy dependency will never last or be fruitful spiritually.

When a woman can learn to connect to her husband through Christ-like affection and a shared intimacy with Jesus, this is when the marriage will be the strongest. The ideal is for both husband and wife to meet at the cross. Through having a firm foundation in their relationship with God, both men and women can be sustained and can *then* experience fulfilling joy and satisfaction in their marriage. But the truth is, many women are married to men who are not walking on God's path. If this is you, that does not leave you off the holy woman list. It just means these words of Scripture are that much more for *you*. Adorn yourself—not with the love and admiration of your husband, not with an outward display of a marriage that is super-spiritual, and certainly not with the anger or resentment of a scorned woman, but with hope and trust in the Lord. Then you will be holy, beautiful, and precious in the eyes of the Lord.

Reflection

- Journal about a time when you felt betrayed by a man (men) in your life. How has your lack of trust in men led you to struggle in your life?
- How have trust issues affected your mental health, emotional well-being, or even your physical health?
- Often when a woman struggles to trust people, she tends to resist trusting God too, perhaps doubting that He is good, loving, and faithful. Instead, she wonders whether He will betray her as the people in her life have done. Have you had this experience?
- How do you believe your life would change or has already changed because of putting your *full trust* in the Lord?

Jessica Rothmeyer PhD

DAY TWO

A Picture of Submission

*For in this way the holy women of former times, who hoped in God, also used to adorn themselves, **being subject to their own husbands,** just as Sarah obeyed Abraham, calling him lord; and you have proved to be her children if you do what is right without being frightened by any fear* (1 Peter 3:5–6 NASB).

Here we are in week three, and I am afraid it is time to talk about the dreaded topic of submission. I am, of course, being somewhat facetious by saying it this way, but after teaching on this topic for many years, I have heard plenty of sighs, groans, and rebuttals. I realize that being submissive to your husbands can be a sore subject. So many factors play into this mighty and complex dynamic in marriage. We know that Scripture calls men to be the head of the family, yet we see many areas of our modern lives where women are leading: in parenting, in schooling, in spirituality, and sometimes even in income. And what happens if a husband is totally uninvolved in the family, behaving in an ungodly manner, or being unkind, even to the point of being verbally abusive? Is a wife still called to be submissive? Believe me, I have heard all the arguments.

If we reflect on women of old, they lived in a very different culture and a completely different political atmosphere than we do today. In biblical times, men regarded women as gentle and sensitive, a gender to be revered and protected. It was common for Hebrew men to leave the room and gather in a public place, away from their wives, when discussing politics, war, death, or any type of stressful topic, so as not to upset God's "gentle creatures." That is certainly not the case anymore. Women are expected to not only handle stressful situations and the harshest of conversations, but they are also now expected to be leaders and problem-solvers of this world's most hostile circumstances.

And then we wonder why women are depressed, anxious, and more stressed mentally and emotionally than ever before. We must take God's truth and apply it to our lives *today*, while also reflecting on what would be the righteous lifestyle He intended for women. God's Word is timeless. He does not change. His Word does not change. Although our lives and the society we live in today does not look a bit like those of old, His truth still stands unwavering. So, what do we do with verses like these that encourage us to behave submissively, like the holy women of old, giving the example of how Sarah obeyed her husband Abraham?

In order to align your mindset with the Kingdom, it is important to first reflect on how God has called the husband to be the *example* by loving his wife like Christ loved the church and gave his life for her. This was Abraham's calling. He was held under great authority and expectation by the Lord to behave in a Godly and righteous manner. And Abraham had a healthy fear and reverence for the Father of the universe. And then, as we learned last week, if husbands choose to not obey God's Word, their wives are to approach them and their conflict with them in a kind, gentle, and peaceable way. That is how *Jesus reacted* to those who were not behaving in Godly ways toward Him, who were exhibiting words and behaviors that were displeasing to God.

As a counselor, I have worked with many women who have wounds from their churches, pastors, and other Christian women who have told them they "should just submit" to their husbands, no matter how they were being treated, but that is not what this verse is saying. In marriage, both husband and wife must do their part. If you are or have been married to either a non-believing husband or to one who claims to be Christian, but is unkind to you for many years, and you believe you have tried to love him like Jesus, and you have prayed for wisdom in how to be a Godly wife, then you have done your part. Your heavenly Daddy sees you as a precious and delicate daughter, and it is *not* His will for women to be battered, controlled, and forced into submission. This is not the definition of *Godly submission*.

But I believe this is a *very small* percentage of the population. Most couples I have encountered and counseled begin their marriage with good will and good intentions toward one another, and it is only over time that they begin to grow apart, becoming wounded by unresolved conflict or experiences of significant stress or trauma. The wounds and distance then cause them to treat one another poorly. In these cases, one or both of the spouses can dramatically change the marital atmosphere by being submissive to one another's needs. This biblical advice is not just for wives. And it must all come from the motivation to be like Jesus, following in His example: *"Submit to one another out of reverence for Christ"* (Eph. 5:21 NIV).

Jesus set the example, over and over, of how to be submissive by being under the authority of Father God during His time here on earth. If Jesus can be submissive, then so can we. There were times when Jesus struggled too. Being kind and forgiving when others hate you, betray you, and try to kill you isn't easy. But because of the love of His Father and the future of humanity, Jesus obeyed and submitted. He submitted over and over out of love for us. This is the example the women of old were setting for us, the future generations. They served and honored their husbands (despite how their husbands might have been acting) out of love for the Father.

Learning the spiritual power in submission has been one of my greatest *personal* breakthroughs, spiritually and emotionally. In times when I want to be done in my marriage, in ministry, or in parenting, I simply submit these issues back to God and have faith that His will and grace is bigger than my own efforts. Trusting He knows what is best for me and my loved ones, my job is to continue to forgive, repent for *my part* in the issues of life, stay humble, and pray.

Viewing submission through a Kingdom lens is very different from a worldly lens. Independent, successful, and "liberated" women of today can find this word difficult to swallow, much less embrace it as a power move, but it is. In fact, submission is one of the most spiritually influential characteristics Jesus demonstrated. He left His position in the triune Godhead in Heaven to become a human. (Yuck!) He came as a baby and had to go through all the humbling stages of childhood. And then He worked, sweated, walked, went hungry, and did all the human things we do so that He could demonstrate how to love and serve others. Finally, He gave His life for us in the most brutal way so we could be forgiven and have eternal life. His submission to the Father, living those 33 years of sacrifice for our benefit, conquered sin and death for all eternity. I'd say submission is pretty powerful.

On a much smaller scale, yet still thoroughly impressive, I have seen many miracles happen in marriages through the Christ-like submission of a wife who chooses to respect and serve a spouse who does not *deserve it*. She forgives when it breaks her heart to do so. She seeks God with all she is so she can be sustained until her husband comes to his senses and chooses to love her as he should, as God's Word instructs. A wife's mercy and grace-filled behaviors can change a man. Godly submission is life changing.

Reflection

- What are some ways you have tried to be submissive?
- Have you found you are able to do so with a content heart, or are there times when you have had to pray about how to react and have a submissive attitude in your relationship? Discuss these struggles.
- In specific ways, how was the life of Jesus an inspiration to you in the past, or how will you use it in the future to help with your motivation in being submissive to your husband and Father God?
- Do you believe you have a healthy view of what Godly submission looks like—such as beneficial boundaries, assertive yet respectful communication, and knowing when to stay silent without harboring resentment?
- The topic of submission has been distorted by many doctrines, as well as falsely taught by worldly standards. Seek God's version of submission by asking the Holy Spirit to reveal the truth to you through reading Scripture such as those listed in today's study.

DAY THREE

Daughters of Sarah

*For in this way the holy women of former times, who hoped in God, also used to adorn themselves, being subject to their own husbands, **just as Sarah obeyed Abraham,** calling him lord; and you have proved to be her children if you do what is right without being frightened by any fear* (1 Peter 3:5–6 NASB).

Am I the only one that feels a little inadequate when reading Scripture about the Godly women of old, like the super-holy woman of Proverbs 31? Do you ever feel unworthy to be called righteous and redeemed? Mostly, I wonder how many Christian women learn to *fully walk* in their holiness by overcoming the lies and false teachings of this world that whispers, "You are not enough."

Reading verse 6, which says we are to be like Sarah, it might seem easy to be discouraged in comparing ourselves to the mother of *all generations*, but let us not forget *all of* who Sarah was. She was indeed a holy woman, called by God for a *very special* reason and purpose, but she had her human weaknesses and not-so-great moments, too. Sarah told her husband Abraham to sleep with another woman when she did not become pregnant in her desired timing. Then later, she wanted him to banish that woman, Hagar, and his son, Ishmael, and she resented Abraham and Hagar for being together. And finally, *she laughed* when God said she would become pregnant at 80 years of age. The truth is, life, faith, parenting, and marriage are *hard*. It's okay to be human, to have a bad day, to be moody with your husband, or to become frustrated with your kids. You can *still* be used by God and regarded as a *holy* woman.

Many times during my spiritual journey, I have questioned whether my words and behaviors were pleasing to God. Sometimes, it has only been by the conviction of the Holy Spirit that I have realized my words or behaviors were *not* Godly. But more often than not, I can be overwhelmed by striving in my own efforts to make my heavenly Daddy proud. I serve my family; I try to forgive quickly; I make efforts to respect and honor my husband, even when it is difficult. But this is a daily battle. On other days, I want to run, scream, and avoid my family at all costs. When we get to Heaven some day and can sit and have coffee with some of the greats, like Mary, Martha, Ruth, Sarah, and Esther, I don't think they will tell us their lives were easy just because they had a relationship with God. Will they boast that they always had perfect faith and never doubted, never cried, and never wanted to throw in the towel some days? No way. Honestly, I can't wait for that day. How fun it will be to hear their stories and to celebrate all that the holy women of history have accomplished for God's Kingdom!

I would like to encourage and challenge you to consider this: You are *already* holy—not because you try hard, or because of your achievements, or because of the fruit produced by your family or ministry. You are holy because God made you so through the righteousness of Christ.

> *And so, dear brothers and sisters, you are now made holy, and each of you is invited to the feast of your heavenly calling. So, fasten your thoughts fully onto Jesus, whom we embrace as our Apostle and King-Priest* (Hebrews 3:1–2 TPT).

So, when this verse calls women to be like Sarah who obeyed her husband, remember that she struggled too. Throughout my counseling career, I have listened as women became discouraged, wondering if God heard their cries, questioning whether their marriage would ever improve, and asking how they can forgive their husbands while their own heart is breaking. Dear sister in Christ, I want to encourage you with this, *God sees you and your efforts*. And as we learned in week one of this study,

Father God cares *most* about your heart. If you have righteous intentions and faithful acts of service toward your husband, your family, and your community, He will reward you. Sometimes it will be through a healing in your marriage, and sometimes it will be in overwhelming joy and peace amidst the storm. Either way, God is there for you, and He will sustain you. He is pleased with your submission, your sacrifice, and your suffering, which is never ever wasted.

> *I the Lord search the heart and examine the mind, to reward each person according to their conduct, according to what their deeds deserve* (Jeremiah 17:10 NIV).

Reflection

- Take some time to reflect on the ways you have felt unworthy to be called holy. How have you tried in your own efforts to be kind, submissive, and self-sacrificing, only to be left feeling alone and bitter?
- Have you found a way to see your role as a modern-day holy woman, a daughter of Sarah, as a privilege and calling from God? God is more concerned with you becoming more like *Him* than with your daily comfort or current circumstances. How do you feel about this?
- Are there areas that you now realize the Lord is calling you to realign, in your mind or in your heart, so that they match His Kingdom perspective?

DAY FOUR

Call Him Lord

*For in this way the holy women of former times, who hoped in God, also used to adorn themselves, being subject to their own husbands, just as Sarah obeyed Abraham, **calling him lord;** and you have proved to be her children if you do what is right without being frightened by any fear* (1 Peter 3:5–6 NASB).

Today's study will be a challenge. Without a Kingdom perspective, it could be easy to feel offended and want to dismiss this part of Scripture all together. So, please give me a few paragraphs to explain. A significant part of my efforts in helping my counseling clients find mental, emotional, and spiritual freedom was to teach them about the unhealthy belief systems or worldly doctrines that had caused them ungodly pain, oppression, or bondage in life. For example, one thing our modern world has taught us is that women can do *anything* men can do. The introduction and political push of women's liberation, from the 1920s onward, in the United States had good intentions.

In many ways, it is God's heartbeat that women would be treated fairly, with respect and genuine regard for their talents and abilities to lead, invent, and heal the world. In many ways, women *are equal* to men (which we will study during week four). God designed men and women with different attributes for significant purposes and Kingdom assignments. But there was also a parallel evil agenda to the women's liberation movement. Much of the unrest, stress, and discontent women suffer in our modern world, comes from striving to fulfill roles they were not intended to fill. For example, women were not designed to be a sole provider or a single parent; they are not designed to work full-time and be the spiritual leader, primary parent, and decision-maker in the family. No wonder women have more mental health issues and chronic illnesses today than ever before in history!

Because of the indoctrination of certain worldviews, a type of rebellious spirit can sneak into the mindsets of women, even those with mature faith. This spirit promotes feelings of distress (rather than peace) when trying to accept and live out a Godly feminine identity. God designed women to be loving, nurturing, and servant-hearted. These were characteristics Jesus displayed on a daily basis during His ministry years here on earth, so by His example, it automatically makes these attributes holy and righteous. When this Scripture says Sarah called her husband, Abraham, "lord" (with a lower-case *l*), it simply represents the relationship God calls each believer into—one of submission. Jesus was in constant submission to His Father in Heaven.

In Genesis, Scripture establishes Adam as the leader in the family. That did not lower Eve's place or value in the eyes of Father God. Rather, she was now taking on a *vital* and Christ-like role of being submissive to her husband, but really it was unto the Lord. Adam must also be submissive to the Lord and is held accountable to God for this leadership position. Many people read their Bibles and see this word *lord* and associate it with old language, a title held by a person of royalty in ancient times. But then, we also use this word frequently when referring to God and to Jesus in our prayers. "O Lord, hear my prayers." "You are the Lord and leader of my life, Jesus." But not many fully comprehend the meaning of this title. The word *lord* actually means: "master, a master of slaves."

If calling your husband *lord* wasn't bad enough, how about calling him your *master*? Yikes! That is why we must put on our Kingdom lenses and really understand what God is trying to establish. If you think about it, we are all slaves to something. Slaves to our jobs, our schedules, or our debt. Jesus was completely indebted as a slave to His Father in Heaven, doing God's will, not His own, and offering up the ultimate sacrifice of His life *by His Master's request.* Because we are usually indoctrinated more by the world than by biblical teaching, any talk of slavery is seen as very negative and cruel, as a reality that should not exist. But some form of slavery has always existed since the Fall in the Garden. Originally, Adam and Eve were free and had intimate and supernatural relationship with God, but once they chose to eat from the forbidden tree, they (and all future generations) instantly signed up to be in bondage to a world that was no longer a paradise. It was full of temptation, pain, and suffering.

God is a King, and all kingdoms need to have order and establish certain ranks, hierarchies, and authority to prevent chaos. So, God says, "I am the Lord of it all." Then, as the hierarchy continues, there is Jesus. When Jesus took the form of a man, He submitted to Father God and *fulfilled* the spiritual law to cover sin for all humankind by the shedding of His blood and the resurrection. In this way, He then conquered death for all eternity. After Jesus, in this system of hierarchy comes men, husbands, and fathers who must submit to Jesus first in order to receive their salvation and become righteous through Christ before Father God. They are called to continually submit to their role of headship under God and to lead with *servant-like* and God-honoring intention toward their wives and families.

Then women, wives, and mothers are to submit to their husbands (if they have one, otherwise it is to Jesus, the Bridegroom to us all), because this is the order God established in His Kingdom. In any situation, submission should be viewed as an act of serving and obeying Father God. Was Jesus considered inferior in value or in His spiritual power because He submitted to His Father? Quite the opposite. As women, we must keep this in mind in times when submission is difficult and could cause a wife to feel dismissed, unloved, or unworthy. God sees *you*. Submission is a valuable and highly honored act of obedience to Father God, and it is well-rewarded. Jesus is still reaping the rewards of His submission to this day, and so will you for all of eternity. Just like Sarah, your submission today will affect future generations, which will lead to exponential results and fruit for the Kingdom of God!

Reflection

- What are some of the more difficult aspects of submission for you?
- What kind of words, actions, and intentions do you see from your spouse or family that make submission a questionable step in your

mind? For example, "Should I submit to this, or am I allowing unhealthy behaviors or being co-dependent?"

- Do you have times of confirmation from the Holy Spirit to look back on? Discuss with others.
- I encourage you to be prayerful about your submission, first to God and then to others. He will lead you in the way that you should go if you ask Him.

DAY FIVE

Love Casts Out Fear

*For in this way the holy women of former times, who hoped in God, also used to adorn themselves, being subject to their own husbands, just as Sarah obeyed Abraham, calling him lord; and **you have proved to be her children if you do what is right without being frightened by any fear*** (1 Peter 3:5–6 NASB).

Doing what is right in marriage, in parenting, and in life is easier said than done. Whether in my own experience, or in hundreds of marriage counseling case studies, I have seen that at times doing what is right can be very scary. For example: Staying in a marriage when you question if your husband will ever really meet your needs. Letting go of a rebellious adult child when you fear they will not make it on their own. Taking care of a parent who has hurt you over and over. Choosing to serve when you are tired. Respecting your husband when his behaviors do not warrant it. Sacrificing for children who are constantly ungrateful.

But this line of Scripture carries a crucial biblical truth: We are to do what is right *because of our faith*, without succumbing to our human, fear-based tendencies. Where can you find the strength to do this mighty act of holiness? It is in the Lord and through *His* love for you, which will cast out any fear that holds you back from doing what is right. So often you will hear people say that the opposite of fear is faith, but Scripture reassures us that it is actually *love* that defies fear. Let us begin by studying the verses made famous by modern wedding ceremonies:

> *Love is patient, love is kind, it is not jealous; love does not brag, it is not arrogant. It does not act disgracefully, it does not seek its own benefit; it is not provoked, does not keep an account of a wrong suffered, it does not rejoice in unrighteousness, but rejoices with the truth; it keeps every confidence, it believes all things, hopes all things, endures all things* (1 Corinthians 13:4–7 NASB).

These verses show the depth of the love God has for *us*, the same kind of love that we are to show others, especially our spouses. If one were to really take to heart the full challenge of these verses, it is quite humbling. On those days when you feel hurt, offended, or neglected, do you truly keep no record of wrongs? Do you honestly have *no hint* of jealousy when your husband shows greater affection for your kids, the dog, or his hunting buddies than he shows you? Do you walk in faith, hope, and persevere for long periods of time when your life circumstances seem quite bleak? This is *divine love*. This is the kind of love God is asking you, the modern-day holy woman, to display.

Why is demonstrating this level of grace-filled love so important? Because each believer is called to this position so that through love God may be seen here on this earth, embodied in a person, just like Christ demonstrated. Your motivation is simply knowing that God loves you at this *divine* level and in an even greater capacity than you could ever hope to comprehend. Isn't it interesting that love is the emphasis in 1 Corinthians 13:13, *"But now faith, hope, and love remain, these three; but the greatest of these is love."* Love is the greatest, because God *is* love. Love is the key to health and vitality in this life and will be the very essence of our lives in Heaven. We must learn to abide in God's love *first* so that we can love others from a place of grace, mercy, and never-ending forgiveness.

We have come to know and have believed the love which God has for us. God is love, and the one who remains in love remains in God, and God remains in him. By this, love is perfected with us, so that we may have confidence in the day of judgment; because as He is, we also are in this world. There is no fear in love, but perfect love drives out fear, because fear involves punishment, and the one who fears is not perfected in love. We love, because He first loved us (1 John 4:16–19 NASB).

These verses hold such important truth about our faith journey: It is only through receiving the love of Christ that any of us can hope to have a Godly impact on the lives of those around us. We simply cannot do it through our own efforts. I have walked out this journey with great grief and suffering in my own life, only to come to the end of myself and find that my healing and salvation and the future of my marriage were contingent on the depth of my ability to *remain in the love of God*. If I could spend alone time with Him, be anchored in His Word, and be vigilant to the voice and leadings of the Holy Spirit, then and only then, could I be truly Christ-like to those around me. Only remaining in the love of God enables me to serve, submit, and sacrifice from a deep, deep well of love and mercy that will never run dry. When you experience God's overwhelming and all-encompassing love, you will not fear for your future, the condition of your marriage, or the circumstances of your loved ones, because *you know* you can trust in the Lord for every good thing to come to fruition. And sometimes, He will do so through you in order to show Himself in human form. What an honor!

Reflection

- In your relationships and in your life personally, what do you fear most?
- Have you had an experience in which an encounter with God has settled your mind, heart, and fears in a supernatural way, in a way no amount of striving could?

- If not, how will you pursue God's love in a way in which you might encounter *that kind* of love?
- Do you pursue His presence in times when you feel weary? It is the best fuel to keep us going, enabling us to truly be loving and Christ-like to others when our own efforts run dry.

WEEK FOUR

The Servant Leader

You husbands in the same way, live with your wives in an understanding way, as with someone weaker, since she is a woman; and show her honor as a fellow heir of the grace of life, so that your prayers will not be hindered (1 Peter 3:7 NASB).

Throughout Scripture, God lays out the foundational principle that all followers of Christ are called to be servants—both men and women, both young and old. This week we will take a deeper look at the role God has given to men, husbands, and fathers in 1 Peter 3. In order to be considered a Christ-like head of the household or the leader of his family, a husband must learn to be a *servant leader*. In the ancient times of royal leadership, both good kings and evil kings ruled through different periods of Israel's history. The key characteristic of an evil king is selfishness. An evil king would treat the people of his kingdom poorly and use them in order to gain more wealth and power for himself. But the principal attribute of every *good king* was a very different view of his kingdom and its people: "I am empowered with leadership, talents, and wealth so that I can serve and protect my people, generously distributing provision in a way that enables all my people to thrive." All men are called to be *good kings*, servant leaders to their wives, families, and communities. I highly recommend reading this week's study (all five days) *with your husband,* if he is willing.

DAY ONE

The Emotional Caregiver

You husbands in the same way, live with your wives in an understanding way, as with someone weaker, since she is a woman; and show her honor as a fellow heir of the grace of life, so that your prayers will not be hindered (1 Peter 3:7 NASB).

After facilitating marriage counseling for over twenty years, something I have discussed with *each and every couple* is the idea that men must *learn* to become emotional caregivers. This means being supportive and offering comfort, even when he does not *understand* his wife or her needs. This role often is not instinctual for men, unless they had a really great relationship with their mother or have dedicated significant effort toward becoming a good listener and learned how to express their emotional support to others. For most husbands, the emotional realm is the most difficult aspect of their marriage, and many try to avoid it, causing their wives a great deal of pain and rejection.

But God calls men to be *understanding* in the verses we are studying this week. Often Scripture instructs humans in the ways of life that are good and righteous, though they are not always instinctual. For husbands, in this verse, God is emphasizing the importance of their spiritual and emotional role in marriage—learning to be understanding of their wives. This is so crucial that this verse actually says that if husbands are not living with their wives in a Christ-like way, their prayers will not be answered.

That is some serious business. I could tell you hundreds of testimonies of men who did not know this Kingdom principle before going through our Divine Marriage program, but once they aligned their hearts and minds with God's heart in this area and learned to be more understanding, gentle, and emotionally caring for their wives, miracles happened. For some, they simply began to *enjoy* their wife and their marriage. For others, they experienced increased financial blessing or success in their careers. I have even witnessed physical healings in one or both spouses because of a husband's willingness to be obedient and become his wife's emotional caregiver.

Both the Passion Translation and the Message Bible offer further explanation of this week's verse:

> *Husbands, you in turn must treat your wives with tenderness, viewing them as feminine partners who deserve to be honored...* (1 Peter 3:7 TPT).

> *The same goes for you husbands: Be good husbands to your wives. Honor them, delight in them* (1 Peter 3:7 MSG).

When a husband can adjust his mindset about his wife—realizing she is not overly emotional, crazy, or broken, but that God made her different for a reason—and also begin to fulfill his role as his wife's emotional caregiver, he will *delight* in her. He will have tenderness for her, knowing she is precious and valuable in God's eyes and deserves to be honored and cherished.

This type of Kingdom thinking and understanding of biblical roles typically is not taught in our schools or Hollywood movies or witnessed in many families. Women are told to be strong and unemotional, told they can live out the attributes and roles God assigned to men with no ill effects. But in biblical times, women were revered as gentle and sweet spirits, holy and precious, someone a man should protect and treat with delicate care. Every woman craves (whether she realizes it or not) to be treated like the princess and daughter of the King that she is.

If a woman's spiritual and emotional needs are not met, if her husband speaks to her harshly or dismissively, or if her husband expects her to be an emotionless drone, they will have no hope of establishing a mutually satisfying or God-honoring marriage. When a husband allows his wife to cope with and handle her negative emotions alone and does not cover her in prayer, it not only gravely damages the marital relationship, but it also leaves a wife more open to spiritual attacks in her mind and emotions. If only the world taught husbands the important and *still* valiant role they are to fulfill as their wife's spiritual and emotional knight in shining armor (best dressed in the armor of God).

Some of you might be quietly grieving these Godly qualities you *wished* your husband possessed. I have been giving this biblical counsel to women who feel this way for years: If you are faithful and you fulfill your role as a biblical wife, by loving and honoring your husband, you will acquire great influence to inspire him to be the man you always dreamed he would be and who *God is calling him to be.* Through your righteousness and prayers and by putting your hope and trust in the Lord, you are relinquishing control. You might be surprised at how convincing the Holy Spirit can be to an unsuspecting husband.

Since this is a women's Bible study, you might be thinking, "This is great, but what if my husband isn't reading this?" If he was not interested in reading each day with you, you could consider including him in your homework and reflection questions this week. In my experience, most men are willing to be given education and advice in the area of marriage. Most husbands have very good will toward their marital relationship, but they do not understand the needs of their wives and often feel like they are failing. Therefore, many eventually give up and stop trying at all. Men do not enjoy feeling like a failure. When they try to be emotional caregivers, since it is not instinctual for them, it can leave them feeling very inadequate. Have mercy and grace for your husband, and offer him kind and gentle advice for the specific ways in which he can make you feel loved, heard, and understood.

Reflection

- How have you noticed your husband trying to care for you, but then still missing the mark?
- In what specific ways would you like him to love and care for you, making you feel heard, noticed, and valuable?

- Ask him how it makes him feel to try to be your emotional caregiver? What has he tried, and why doesn't it work from his perspective?
- Share with him specific things you have identified to help him meet your needs in more effective ways. Having to tell your husband *how to care for you* does not take away from his efforts. It is a fantasy to believe men "should just know how to be loving and understanding." It is clear from this week's Scripture that men are unaware of this Kingdom position and fail to realize just how important it is; therefore, they need to be instructed by God to fulfill this essential role in their marriage so that their prayers will not be *hindered.*

DAY TWO

A Prosperous Atmosphere

> *You husbands in the same way, live with your wives in an understanding way,* **as with someone weaker, since she is a woman;** *and show her honor as a fellow heir of the grace of life, so that your prayers will not be hindered* (1 Peter 3:7 NASB).

Peter wasn't exactly being politically correct when calling a woman *weak,* but this word falls into the Kingdom perspective we are trying to establish throughout this study—a gentle femininity that is not to be seen as negative. In Hebrew culture, women were very hard workers, multitasking, a pillar of strength for their families, and relentless in their faith. If you doubt it, read Proverbs 31, which gives a description of a noble and Godly woman. It will challenge everything you have ever thought about the incredible Kingdom significance of being a wife and mother!

In many other translations this word *weaker* is qualified by the adjective *physically.* This verse is speaking to husbands, and these descriptive words fit the lens through which a man sees *his life* (and his fellow brothers)—which can be summed up in two words: *performance driven.* A man feels healthy in his mind and body when he accomplishes tasks, goals, and achievements physically; when he advances in his job, wins at a sport, builds something "with his own two hands," or brings home a "piece of nature" (deer, elk, fish) he has defeated (killed). In this verse, God is trying to help men understand that their wives were not designed like them.

Women might be weaker physically, but they thrive on relationship, not achievements. I wish this latter clarification was added in 1 Peter 3:7, but it is evident in Ephesians 5:25–29:

> *Husbands, love your wives, just as Christ also loved the church and gave Himself up for her, so that He might sanctify her, having cleansed her by the washing of water with the word, that He might present to Himself the church in all her glory, having no spot or wrinkle or any such thing; but that she would be holy and blameless. So, husbands ought also to love their own wives as their own bodies. He who loves his own wife loves himself; for no one ever hated his own flesh, but nourishes and cherishes it, just as Christ also does the church.*

As a marriage counselor I have taught on this passage many times. I have also attended several marriage conferences that used both 1 Peter 3 and Ephesians 5 as important Scriptures for guiding couples in how to have a biblical marriage. Yet I rarely hear someone teach on the atmosphere a husband is to provide for his wife, so that she may be healthy and holy and thrive in life.

Ephesians 5:25 instructs husbands to *love their wives like Christ loved the church.* That is a tall and actually impossible order. For all believers, attaining perfection in being *exactly like* Christ is unachievable, but striving to be Christ-like is a noble effort. I say this, because often wives need to examine the expectations they have for their husbands. Even if your husband is a Christian and mature in his faith, *he will fall short* in his Christ-like performance at times (see Rom. 3:23). That is why a wife must look to Jesus as her spiritual husband when her needs are not being met by her spouse.

Ephesians 5 states Christ washed the church clean, sanctifying her and making her holy by His sacrifice. These Christ-set examples instruct husbands to be serving and sacrificial, to be willing to suffer personally for the benefit of their wives, and to create an environment that enables their wives to be healthy—just as any person would do for their *own* sake. A husband's Christ-like sacrifice is actually *adding to* his wife's holiness. Think about what Jesus did for the church, giving us the ability to become sons and daughters of the Most High God through His death and resurrection. Now, Christ-followers are enabled with spiritual power and eternal victory because Jesus rose from the dead. If believers walk in those spiritual truths, which were established through Christ, then they will have confidence and courage to do great things for the Kingdom every day. If a husband creates an atmosphere for his wife that is filled with love, encouragement, protection, and the reassurance that he will always be by her side emotionally and spiritually, consider how much healthier this woman will be.

Unfortunately, because women have become ultra-independent (due to what society promotes) and given in to the expectation that they must be stronger, smarter, and more energetic than any previous generation of women, they have now stepped outside of their biblical role and Kingdom calling. Look around. How is this worldly mindset working out for women? As a professional counselor, I can attest that most women have never been so unhealthy, mentally, emotionally, physically, or spiritually. Yet, some social and political platforms declare the need for *more* rights and liberation for women, which produces more pressure, responsibility, and weight that can distract women from God's true destiny for their lives.

When a person, male or female, tries to operate outside of their God-given identity, biblical role, gifts, or talents, it always leaves them feeling discontent and exhausted. God destined us to have an abundant life and to accomplish much for His Kingdom, but we must all fall into place in the ranks of His army and operate within the flow of His grace. If you are willing to do this, aligning your will with God's, it will be the *healthiest* choice (mentally, emotionally, and spiritually) you have ever made, and you will experience a glorious feeling of fulfilment in your soul.

And when I say "fall into your rank," I am not suggesting that in order to be considered a modern-day holy woman you must give up your career, ministry, or passions and start acting weak and ignorant compared to men. Rather, a woman is simply at her best when she can thrive in an atmosphere where she *knows,* when push comes to shove, her husband has her back. This is the ideal marriage atmosphere: A wife can depend on her husband to support her emotionally, pray for her, and sacrifice his needs and desires for the greater good of their marriage and family, and a wife also accepts (submits to) her husband's support and leadership as a form of Godly presence in her life. Most importantly, when her husband is *not fulfilling* his biblical role, she should still have peace and experience success in daily life because of her utter reliance on Jesus as her Rock.

The verses of Ephesians 5 go on to say that a husband is to cherish and nourish his wife like he would *his own body*. This shows that a husband should resist being harsh or abusive, because he would not treat his own body this way. A husband should *definitely* not treat his precious and delicate wife in a harsh or insensitive manner. Think of all the things most of us do every day to ensure we take care of our own bodies. We do simple things like stepping around dangerous items as we walk, dressing appropriately for weather conditions, eating when we're hungry, and resting when we're tired. Those are *basic* survival skills. To truly *cherish* his wife, a husband must read the Bible often to renew his mind, take time to rest and be alone with Father God, pursue times of spiritual and physical retreat, and to seek out fellowship with his brothers in Christ in order to stay strong in faith and to help protect him from evil attacks. These are all important areas for the overall well-being of every believer, but it is especially a God-given *charge* to husbands to steward and provide an *atmosphere and support system* for their wives in which they can truly thrive mentally, emotionally, physically, and spiritually.

Reflection

- In what ways could your husband better provide an atmosphere in which you would thrive mentally, emotionally, physically, and spiritually? Please share these specific needs with him.
- Do you think your husband does this for himself first? How could you encourage him to do so with kind and gentle suggestions? As he experiences this himself, abiding in the Father, he will also be able to provide it for you and your family.
- What are some examples of times when you found your solace in Jesus when your husband's efforts fell short?

DAY THREE

Lead Like Jesus

*You husbands in the same way, live with your wives in an understanding way, as with someone weaker, since she is a woman; **and show her honor** as a fellow heir of the grace of life, so that your prayers will not be hindered* (1 Peter 3:7 NASB).

Husbands are called to love their wives like Christ loves the church. They are the head or leader in the family, just as Christ is the leader of the body of believers. In order to be Godly leaders, to *show their wives honor*, men must first learn, observe, and study how Jesus led. Even in biblical times, many religious leaders and devout Jews did not believe Jesus was the Messiah, because he did not operate how *they thought* the Savior of the world would. He was not commanding of speech or authoritative in behavior. He was not (outwardly) a mighty warrior or a stringent army sergeant. Rather, Jesus was kind, gentle, serving, and selfless. He manifested miracles and radical life-change through His sacrificial love for others.

The most important component of my role as a counselor was to teach people how to think. I would begin by teaching them to have the mind of Christ. From this mindset *alone*, we find true and lasting freedom. Philippians 2:3–8 gives us an overview of how to have the mind of Christ:

Do nothing from selfishness or empty conceit, but with humility of mind regard one another as more important than yourselves; do not merely look out for your own personal

> *interests, but also for the interests of others. Have this attitude in yourselves which was also in Christ Jesus, who, as He already existed in the form of God, did not consider equality with God something to be grasped, but emptied Himself by taking the form of a bond-servant and being born in the likeness of men. And being found in appearance as a man, He humbled Himself by becoming obedient to the point of death: death on a cross* (Philippians 2:3–8 NASB).

When reading through these verses, I can identify four main qualities that Jesus represents and demonstrated to the Church during His life as a human: submission, servanthood, suffering, and sacrifice. This Scripture says that even though Jesus existed in the form of God, He did not regard Himself as an equal to God. Jesus led an earthly, human life in complete submission to His Father in Heaven. In order to lead well, a husband must first learn to submit his life, his will, and his goals and desires to God's call for him, for the benefit of his wife and children. Being submitted to God, for both men and women, is the healthiest place we can be mentally and spiritually. It will bring you peace, and the Holy Spirit will be the guide of your life.

After counseling hundreds of husbands over the years, I have heard many men admit that they need help in the areas of leadership, making decisions, and learning how to have a healthy relationship with their wives and children. Without total surrender and daily submission to Father God, the job of husband and father is nearly impossible. Jesus is *one* with God. He has been present from the beginning of time as the Word. He willingly humbled Himself and gave up His Godhead to become human, and He perfectly demonstrated how to live a submitted life unto His Father in Heaven. If the Holy One of Israel can do it, then no amount of pride or shame should keep a husband from being on his knees daily, asking for the help, wisdom, and direction he needs from the Holy Spirit to live out his biblical role fully *submitted* to Father God.

Second, these verses explain that Jesus took the position of a bondservant. A bondservant, similar to a slave, is a servant who is bonded to a family for life. Bondservants never repay their debts, but gladly and willingly serve their master all the days of their lives. The master, in return, treats the bondservant like one of the family, with respect and love. This is *who Jesus described Himself* to be to His Father, and it is how Peter and Paul later identified themselves in relationship to Jesus Christ.

Husbands are called to be bondservants to the Lord, calling Him master and gladly and willingly obeying Him all the days of their lives. Imagine the strong, Spirit-led marriages and families we would have in the world today if men were willing to be bondservants to Christ. Some already are, just as some women are seeking to be modern-day holy women, but I think we could all agree that it is a small percentage. Part of why Jesus came to this earth was to set the example for how believers should relate to their Father in Heaven. For many men, having a servant-like attitude at work or even with friends or strangers is their second nature. Many men receive a great deal of satisfaction (and often much-needed accolades) for their efforts to help and be gracious to others, but when it comes to those closest to them, their wives and children, serving can be a forgotten role in their daily lives.

Jesus served His mother Mary. He always had time for the widow, the tax collector, and the prostitute. He humbly washed the feet of His disciples. Jesus served His loved ones, His friends, and those in the community with *equal commitment and fervor.* These verses go on to say how Jesus suffered for our sake. Jesus not only suffered the most brutal beating and death on the cross, but He suffered daily in ways He would not have if He had kept His divine position in Heaven. Jesus had to grow up in a very different world than His previous home in Heaven, suffering through all the developmental stages of childhood. His parents even yelled at Him, scolding Him for wandering off on His own, even though He was just doing what He knew He was called to do, spending dedicated time alone with His Father (see Luke 2:41–52).

Jesus suffered in many ways during His life on earth; He was often hungry, criticized, lied about, condemned, and in the end, crucified. He chose all of these sufferings so that the generations to come would inherit eternal life with Him in Heaven. Only when we mediate on Christ's suffering, done out of love *for us,* will we be motivated to suffer for others. Because of the false teachings in this modern world, many people avoid suffering at all cost. People have become very selfish and self-centered, with life goals focused on achieving material wealth and having fun. They look to all kinds of creature comforts to help soothe any hint of pain or feelings of discontent. Both men and women are called to suffer (more on this topic next week), but as God calls men to *lead like Jesus*, a Godly husband must take a deeper look into the specific ways the Holy Spirit might be asking *him to suffer* for the health, wellness, and overall survival of his wife and children.

Finally, Jesus sacrificed His life so that we can be called righteous and redeemed before Father God. Without the shedding of His blood for our sins, we could never achieve salvation on our own, so we are forever indebted to Christ for this holy and eternal gift. Ephesians 5:25 specifically says men are to give up their lives for their wives as Christ gave His life for the Church. God *designed men* to do this. It is why little boys want to be police officers, fire-fighters, soldiers, and superheroes. A man has an instinctual desire to sacrifice for the greater good, to give his life (on some level) so that others can be safe and prosper. When a husband denies this Godly role, it leads him to become very unhealthy and unfulfilled. Becoming your husband's cheerleader can breathe new life into an otherwise hopeless and weary man. He needs to know his sacrificial deeds are not going unnoticed. He needs to know he is still your knight in shining armor, your modern-day superhero.

Reflection

- Talk to your husband today about these four roles: submission, serving, suffering, and sacrifice—roles *all believers* are called to fulfill. Build him up by sharing how you admire how he has displayed each of these areas for you, your children, or his community.
- Journal and then share *your personal struggles* in each of these areas: submission, servanthood, suffering, and sacrifice. Open up the conversation by being the first to expose *your* vulnerable weaknesses. Vulnerability gives way to vulnerability, and every wife yearns to have a husband who is open and shares his true feelings. Since women are the relationship experts, *you go first*.
- Gently and with positive encouragement tell him how he could demonstrate something specific in each of these areas, so that you and your children can more significantly recognize his provision, protection, and love.

DAY FOUR

Equality in Christ

*You husbands in the same way, live with your wives in an understanding way, as with someone weaker, since she is a woman; and show her honor **as a fellow heir of the grace of life**, so that your prayers will not be hindered* (1 Peter 3:7 NASB).

In the short piece of Scripture we study today, you will see God's heart for equality. It is a reminder to husbands that, although God places them in a role of leadership in the marriage and family, in God's eyes, husband and wife, man and woman, are equals. In fact, this truth is even more broadly established, in that *all believers*, no matter their race, gender, age, or past sins, are seen as equal, because God *only sees* the righteousness of Christ in us. *"For there is no partiality with God"* (Rom. 2:11).

This is your incredible inheritance: Because of what Jesus did at the cross, and by your faith and decision to make Jesus the Lord and Savior of your life, you are seen as perfect and holy before Father God. This is the magnificent miracle of the **grace of life** (which is everlasting). Gender and race equality have been controversial social issues for many generations, but in the Kingdom of God, we are all equal *because of Jesus.* If we could see each other through the eyes of Christ, people would treat one another so differently.

That is God's reminder to husbands here, to see their wives as those who deserve great honor and should be treated with equality, *even if* they are more emotional or physically weaker than their husbands. What man sees often is not what is important to God (as we discussed in regard to outward beauty); rather, God cares about our hearts. In Genesis, when Scripture says God created humans, it says He created them in His image. It then clarifies that God set them apart, male and female, *both* made in His image, yet with different and equally holy attributes. *"God created man in His own image, in the image of God He created him; male and female He created them"* (Gen. 1:27).

When my husband and I co-facilitate marriage coaching, we spend a great deal of time with our clients discussing the *value and specific design* of God's assignment in who He created both a husband and a wife to be. Both have equal destinies and purpose in God's Kingdom. It is also important to observe that when God created Eve, He took a rib from Adam's *side*, an image of equality and intention, as they are to walk *side by side* in life. There is no superiority in that image. And let us not forget that Adam was created from the dust and to dust we shall *all* return (see Gen. 3:19). This is humbling, and hopefully it inspires each Jesus-follower to stay in a place of submission and gratitude for the incredible *grace* our mighty God shows us every day. Let us never take for granted the life He has given us and the eternal salvation Jesus won for us by His death and resurrection!

Finally, let's remember that we are *all called* to submit to one another out of reverence for Christ (see Eph. 5:21). Let this be a constant reminder of who Christ is and how *we* are to be examples of His love and character, demonstrating Kingdom principles in our daily interactions, because *the world is watching.* So, as husbands, men are called to submit to the needs of their wives in Godly ways, not because it is easy, not to emasculate them or cause them to feel inadequate, but because of their love and reverence for Christ. And wives, you are called to submit to your husbands in Godly ways, not because he deserves it or because you are a doormat, but because of your love and reverence for Christ. The world might have convinced you that being submissive is synonymous with being weak, but in the Kingdom, submission is *spiritually powerful,* and it takes very strong and faith-filled people to live lives of Christ-like submission, remembering their spouses are *equal heirs* in the grace of life.

Reflection

- Journal and discuss with your husband ways in which you have seen him treat you as an equal heir to the grace of life.
- Bring to light any areas in which you have felt "less than" in your marital relationship.
- Pray about it first, to see if this is your perception based on past wounds caused by others (the world) or if you need to seek resolution and forgiveness between you and your spouse.
- Challenge yourself to see the Godly attributes in one another, as husband and wife, so that you can celebrate more, recognizing you are both created equal and *yet different*, set apart as male and female, for a reason and a very *specific* purpose in God's Kingdom.

DAY FIVE

Serious Business

*You husbands in the same way, live with your wives in an understanding way, as with someone weaker, since she is a woman; and show her honor as a fellow heir of the grace of life, **so that your prayers will not be hindered*** (1 Peter 3:7 NASB).

When I read the last phrase of this verse, I cannot help but think to myself, "Don't mess with God's daughters!" Although our Father in Heaven is good and merciful, and He gives us so much more love and grace than we deserve, sometimes His warnings and admonishments are necessary. That's just good parenting. The entirety of verse seven contains some very powerful Kingdom principles that we have now taken four days to establish. But in the grand scheme of life, it is vital for a husband to understand the spiritual law found in these last eight words of verse 7: If a husband does not honor his wife, God may not answer his prayers. Wow.

In order to not misinterpret these words, it is crucial to view your life and all those with whom you interact through a Kingdom lens. The Kingdom of God has spiritual laws and rules by which all creation must abide. The angels and demons who reside in the spiritual realm know these rules well and *must* operate within them. The Father created all the angels (even the ones who rebelled, choosing to follow Satan and become his dark army), and God is just and never-changing, so He always enforces the Kingdom rules. In Jesus' time here on earth, He lived in full submission to these spiritual laws and practiced them to perfection, especially when He fulfilled the greatest of them all by becoming the perfect Lamb as a sacrifice for sin, creating a new covenant offering salvation and eternal life through faith in Him. Humans on the other hand, typically do *not* understand how the spiritual realm operates. Studying the Bible and nurturing an intimate relationship with the Holy Spirit is our only hope in gaining wisdom and experiencing spiritual victory in this life.

God gave Moses the ten commandments in the Old Testament as guidelines to help His people think and behave correctly. Throughout biblical times, God sent holy men and women to be teachers and prophets and to remind people of the ways of His Kingdom. Then the Father gave the world His one and only Son to set all His children free from sin and condemnation, but He never removed the guidelines. God's desire is for each believer to be continually refined to become more and more like Christ. This refinement is necessary, so that we can become image bearers of who *He is* to the world around us, so that others might come to know and believe in Him because of how we live our lives—in a holy and righteous manner.

With all of that said, if a husband (or wife) does not show Christ-like behavior toward his (or her) spouse, if a man does not offer his wife love and understanding as God has called him to, then his prayers may be hindered. This is not because God wants to punish us or because we have to follow a set of rules so that we can get our way; rather, it is because God is most concerned with our *hearts*. He is always conditioning us to think and love like He does. Unanswered prayers can be quite motivating. This is an important verse in Scripture that should cause pause and self-reflection in a husband. If specific prayers in his life are not being answered, if he feels a void in his relationship with God, if he does not feel Godly momentum in his business or daily life, he should examine how he is treating his wife. This matters greatly to God, because marriage is a symbol, a representation of who Christ is to the Church.

Christ is the Bridegroom, and the Church is the Bride, and one day when we go to Heaven, we will *only be married to Jesus* (see Matt. 22:30). But here on this earth, we have the opportunity to use the sacred union of marriage to demonstrate the love and sacrificial relationship Christ has with us. As Christians, when we treat each other poorly, abandon our loved ones, betray them, or choose to be self-focused, these behaviors inadvertently communicate to the world a very non-Christian message. It is not always intentional, but it can be a very loud and blatant example of ungodliness. This can cause people to question if Jesus is faithful, if He is *actually* trustworthy and loving. Reflecting on their own life experiences, they might think, "Perhaps Jesus will leave me, too, when the going gets tough." These subliminal messages happen quite frequently in the minds of believers and non-believers alike, all because of what we have witnessed in our human relationships.

Just as an unhealthy marriage can affect the relationship we have with Jesus, childhood experiences with our earthly fathers can drastically affect how we see and interact with Father God. If your father was harsh, dismissive, or loved you based on performance, you will probably view your Heavenly Father that way, unless you find healing for those wounds and truly understand who God is by studying the Word. The same goes for marriage. If your husband ignores you, makes you feel unworthy, or does not meet your emotional needs, you might struggle to find intimacy with Jesus. The world often misunderstands who God and Jesus are, because they view these holy and superior beings through the lens of their own hurts and wounds. They compare the Godhead to the experiences they have had in human relationships. But that is not who our God is. Only through knowing Scripture, along with personal encounters of God's presence, can we feel as *loved* and *fulfilled* as He wants each of His children to feel.

Many people do not seek Him in these ways on their own. Often, observations of or interactions with Christians will cause a seeker to want to know more about Jesus. They wonder what could cause these people to be so kind, so generous. What would cause a father to be so loving to his children? What would cause a husband to demonstrate such care and understanding to his wife? What enables a woman to be strong and brave, yet also gentle and submissive to her husband? These observations will cause the world to say, "Who are these people, and what motivates them to act this way?"

Reflection

- Journal and then discuss with your husband what kind of image and message your marriage is speaking to the world, especially to your children.
- Are there prayers that your husband has expressed (or perhaps you can ask him about his current prayer requests) that might be hindered? Are they Godly prayers that lend to putting his wife and family before his own needs and desires?
- How can you help your husband walk out his role as a servant leader? Does he need your encouragement or gentle reminders? Do you make it a habit to pray together as husband and wife (which is very emotionally bonding and powerful in the spiritual realm)?

WEEK FIVE

Unified with God, Husband, and Church

To sum up, all of you be harmonious, sympathetic, loving, compassionate, and humble; not returning evil for evil or insult for insult, but giving a blessing instead; for you were called for the very purpose that you would inherit a blessing. For, "The one who desires life, to love and see good days, must keep his tongue from evil and his lips from speaking deceit. He must turn away from evil and do good; he must seek peace and pursue it. For the eyes of the Lord are toward the righteous, and His ears attend to their prayer, but the face of the Lord is against evildoers" (1 Peter 3:8–12 NASB).

Although this study is particularly for women, the overall teaching in 1 Peter 3 is holiness and righteousness for *all humankind*. After Peter gives instruction to husbands and wives based on their instinctual weaknesses, he goes on to remind *all believers* how they are to think and behave as citizens of the Kingdom of God. This week we will review common themes we have already discussed: being peacemakers, being kind, resisting provocation, having self-control, not saying negative or hurtful words, being humble, and seeking a righteous lifestyle. It is important for every person to learn the ways of the Kingdom—how to think, act, and feel based on Godly principles, which we will not do instinctually, left to our own fleshly desires, since we live in a dark and fallen world. To radically live out our faith, we must study the Word of God often and be encouraged by fellow believers to stay on the narrow path to holiness and right-living.

> *Enter through the narrow gate; for the gate is wide and the way is broad that leads to destruction, and there are many who enter through it. For the gate is narrow and the way is constricted that leads to life, and there are few who find it* (Matthew 7:13–14 NASB).

DAY ONE

The Upside-Down Kingdom

To sum up, all of you be harmonious, sympathetic, loving, compassionate, and humble; not returning evil for evil or insult for insult, but giving a blessing instead; for you were called for the very purpose that you would inherit a blessing. For, "The one who desires life, to love and see good days, must keep his tongue from evil and his lips from speaking deceit. He must turn away from evil and do good; he must seek peace and pursue it. For the eyes of the Lord are toward the righteous, and His ears attend to their prayer, but the face of the Lord is against evildoers" (1 Peter 3:8–12 NASB).

As you read, study, and become more familiar with the Word of God, you will begin to understand that *Kingdom* principles are not like those of this world. One significant biblical example is the Sermon on the Mount; Speaking to His disciples and the religious leaders, Jesus turned the morals and human laws being taught at that time on their head! To begin to really understand how God thinks and how His Kingdom operates, read through Matthew 5–7 and ask the Holy Spirit to thoroughly open your spiritual eyes and ears to the profound biblical truths found there. As a spiritual counselor, I have seen many, many people set free in their minds and emotions and even healed in their bodies when they came to believe the words written in these three chapters and embraced a Kingdom perspective. For example, Jesus taught: *"Blessed are those who hunger and thirst for righteousness, for they will be satisfied"* (Matt. 5:6).

Many mental health issues are born out of feelings of loneliness, emptiness, dissatisfaction, discontent, and a lack of motivation or purpose in life. But if you ask Jesus to be the Lord and leader of your life and seek to become more and more like Him, you will be satisfied in ways that no amount of love from other humans, fancy vacations, or days at the spa could ever accomplish. When you hunger and thirst for righteousness, your mindset about what is truly important and valuable in life begins to change, and your fleshly desires begin to fade. Your spirit will crave more and more of what God's Kingdom has to offer—like peace, joy, contentment, excitement for eternal life, a fervor and drive to serve others, and a desire to win more souls for Jesus. These thoughts and emotions produce great fruit in your life and in the lives of those around you, fulfilling you in ways you have never imagined. You will be satisfied far beyond what the world and its empty promises ever could offer.

Now that we are beginning to understand how to think and behave like Jesus, we can take a deeper look at the instruction in today's verse—to be harmonious, sympathetic, loving, compassionate, and humble. How often do we see these characteristics in our fellow humans? It is so easy to follow the world's teachings and examples of behavior, becoming confrontational, self-centered, individualistic, self-promoting, and boastful. Especially with the rise in popularity of social media, everyone wants to be a star, to be noticed and famous (or infamous). I see all kinds of people, young and old, male and female, being rude, harsh, and divisive in order to capture a following or receive a few likes and be considered an influencer.

But as believers, we are called to *influence* this world in very different ways. Kingdom ways are self-sacrificing and will not always be noticed, as we discussed earlier in this study. But it is better to be rewarded in Heaven for the things that go unnoticed by this world than to receive the applause or accolades of humans. It can be very hard, especially when we continue to endure the words and behaviors of those who do not *deserve* our sympathetic kindness or harmonious and humble gestures. It can be a great move of God within us to have God-honoring *outward* behaviors and *inward* conviction to live righteously without going down a path of bitterness and resentment. But this is who we are called to be in His Kingdom.

These verses go on to say that, as believers, we are not to repay evil for evil or insult for insult, and even just staying silent is not *enough*. We must offer a blessing to those who hurt or harm us instead. Now that is humbling and refining!

One of the Christ-like attributes we are to exude is that of peacemakers. Jesus said He came to give peace like no other. As a baby, He was regarded as the Prince of Peace. Once you experience the true peace of God, nothing else in this world will satisfy your emotional needs. Nothing will calm and center your soul like *His* peace. Therefore, we are to carry *that peace* out into the world and improve every atmosphere we enter, leaving His peace with others wherever we go. This effort to bring and maintain peace is a step of holiness. And our striving for holiness is in conjunction with our intimate relationship with the Holy Spirit, which keeps us close and in *real, intimate* relationship with the Lord. *"Pursue peace with all people, and the holiness without which no one will see the Lord"* (Heb. 12:14 NASB).

Reflection

- Journal about times when you offered Christ-like blessings to those who did not deserve or warrant them at the time.
- Reflect and discuss how difficult it can be and what kind of mindset you must have in those moments in order to sustain Godly thoughts, feelings, and behaviors in the face of adversity.
- Be honest and repent for times when you responded with your flesh and looked like the world, repaying evil for evil or insult for insult.
- Make a declaration and write out a blessing for those you know who are in need of it today, those who are not yet Kingdom-minded and are looking to *you* to be the example of Christ on this earth.

Jessica Rothmeyer PhD

DAY TWO

Inheritance

To sum up, all of you be harmonious, sympathetic, loving, compassionate, and humble; not returning evil for evil or insult for insult, but giving a blessing instead; **for you were called for the very purpose that you would inherit a blessing.** *For, "The one who desires life, to love and see good days, must keep his tongue from evil and his lips from speaking deceit. He must turn away from evil and do good; he must seek peace and pursue it. For the eyes of the Lord are toward the righteous, and His ears attend to their prayer, but the face of the Lord is against evildoers"* (1 Peter 3:8–12 NASB).

As we read the last line of 1 Peter 3:9, let it be a reminder of the reason *why* we choose to live a holy and righteous lifestyle: We are to inherit the greatest of blessings, eternal life. Any sacrifices we make dim in comparison to what Jesus did on the cross for us and the magnificent reward that awaits us in Heaven.

I have found that, unless we spend time understanding the *love* of Father God and embracing His incredible grace and mercy (which is truly an undeserved, unearned gift because of Jesus), it is difficult to fully realize how costly His sacrifice was and just how blessed we truly are, every day, to *be adopted* into the family of God.

> *He predestined us to adoption as sons and daughters through Jesus Christ to Himself, according to the good pleasure of His will, to the praise of the glory of His grace, with which He favored us in the Beloved* (Ephesians 1:5–6 NASB).

If only we could truly comprehend and then *hold onto* all that these words suggest. We are adopted, made to be a part of the royal and holy family of God through Christ! He sees each of us as one of His own. He favors us. Only through *adoption* are we are able to share in the inheritance of salvation. An inheritance is neither earned nor deserved; it is simply given and passed down to family members. But you *have to* be part of the family to receive this inheritance.

Receiving an inheritance, especially a large sum (again, which you did not earn), brings most people a great deal of humility. Such an abundant gift often causes the receiver to reflect on how they might have mistreated the Giver, the One who is so graciously willing to give them such a priceless gift. Some are left wondering, "Why would He give all that He has for me, someone who has done nothing to deserve it?" Jesus sacrificed His life and His place in Heaven for 33 years, and He endured indescribable suffering *for this inheritance*: To bring many, many children into the family of God.

When I struggle to be kind, sympathetic, or peaceful toward people or situations that have not treated me well, I remember this: Jesus has not received His *full inheritance*, yet. And, if I can, I want to play a part in helping Him receive *all that is due*. And then one day, all believers will share in *that inheritance*, both in reaping the wonderful reward of eternal life and in seeing the many souls of those we ministered to joining us in Heaven. Whether you helped them directly enter into a relationship with Jesus or you simply helped to plant seeds through expressions of Christ-like love, compassion, or mercy, you *will someday know* how valuable your contributions truly are to the overall advancement of God's Kingdom.

Reflection

- How would you act or react differently, keeping in mind that you are a *child of God* who will receive a great inheritance someday? Is this eternal mindset motivation for you?

- How can you use today's lesson as a reminder and a passion-igniter in times when your efforts seem fruitless or ignored?
- Our soul and flesh can become weary, but our Spirit is always ready to harvest a full inheritance, and it will be the most glorious experience when we receive it. Hold onto this truth!

_____

_____

_____

_____

_____

_____

_____

_____

_____

_____

_____

_____

_____

_____

DAY THREE

The Spiritual Power in Words

*To sum up, all of you be harmonious, sympathetic, loving, compassionate, and humble; not returning evil for evil or insult for insult, but giving a blessing instead; for you were called for the very purpose that you would inherit a blessing. **For, "The one who desires life, to love and see good days, must keep his tongue from evil and his lips from speaking deceit.** He must turn away from evil and do good; he must seek peace and pursue it. For the eyes of the Lord are toward the righteous, and His ears attend to their prayer, but the face of the Lord is against evildoers"* (1 Peter 3:8–12 NASB).[4]

As a counselor, I have spent many hours teaching on the mental, emotional, and spiritual power found in our words. This biblical truth is woven throughout Scripture: The words we speak have a creative force. I have watched this spiritual principle play out before my eyes for more than two decades. The words you speak determine your thinking, your feelings, and

---

[4] For the rest of the week, we will be studying Psalm 34:12–17, which Peter quotes here. It holds powerful truth about living a holy and righteous lifestyle, which is Peter's overall message throughout chapter three.

very often your actions and behaviors. Many people do not understand and dramatically underestimate the power of their daily speech.

Our society tends to be very sarcastic and thrives on poking fun at different social groups or individuals with different opinions or cultural views than their own. Many people thrive on social media by making personal attacks and offering their negative comments—some as devasting as death threats, intimidation, or suggesting that people kill themselves. I have personally received such comments, as well as heard these reports from my clients for years, all since the rise of social media platforms and cyber bullying.

The world has trained us to believe our words are basically empty. "I'm just kidding," or "I didn't mean it," people might say. Perhaps it is just a piece of juicy gossip, and you think, "What could it hurt?" Maybe you embellish a conflict or interaction (speaking deceit) in order to gain the favor and validation of your audience. Others will be unapologetic about their harsh words and say that people *deserve* to be told they are stupid, ugly, naughty, selfish, lazy, or fat. But the Word of God warns us that our words have spiritual power, and *we will reap the fruit of what we speak*, good or bad. *"Death and life are in the power of the tongue, and those who love it will eat its fruit"* (Prov. 18:21 NASB).

In our verse for today, it says if you want to *see good days,* you must keep your tongue from speaking evil—both against others and *yourself.* Some of the most awful things I have heard my clients say were the negative words they spoke about themselves. This familiar and self-defeating habit is validated in the world by saying: "They just have poor self-esteem." The world we live in broadcasts a constant barrage of perfectionism promoted by filtered and air-brushed pictures and videos in movies, magazines, and social media. How could anyone ever feel like they are *good enough.* The greatest danger in this social programming is that most people have no clue where to find their value and worth.

From a biblical perspective, let us remember that our value, worth, and identity are *not* found in our outward beauty, in our intelligence or career achievements, or in our marriage or children. True and unshakeable identity can only be found in Christ. From this foundation *alone* can we establish a healthy mind and steadfast emotions. Instead of teaching my clients how to have positive self-talk, as suggested by the world, I teach them to make daily declarations of their Godly attributes by quoting Scripture that states who and whose they are. You can find a list of these declarations in Appendix 2 at the end of this book. I also teach parents to speak these biblical truths over the lives of their children, which teaches them from a young age how to win the battle in their minds and how to protect themselves from any negative speech spoken against them by others.

For many years, I worked primarily with children by providing in-home family counseling. These experiences often left me with a broken heart, but also taught me a very important spiritual lesson. I observed how many children suffered mentally and emotionally because of the *negative words* spoken over their lives by parents, teachers, doctors, and other counselors. I have advised many parents and individuals since that time to be cautious and to ask the Holy Spirit to guard and filter their words every day in order to protect themselves, their children, their spouse, and every person they encounter. This is especially true if you are a person with any type of authority over others. Your words can be a blessing or a curse and can have life-long effects in someone's life.

One way I have seen people's lives dramatically decline as a result of someone's words is through a medical diagnosis. Whether it is physical or psychological, having a professional say, "This is what is wrong with you..." can be oddly comforting. The world has trained us to believe we must *know everything* in order to have peace of mind. But these labels often cause people (or the parents of small people) to begin to curse their own lives with all of the criteria and attributes that come along with a diagnosis. This makes it almost impossible to heal or break free from that diagnosis. For example, a patient might claim, "I have Major Depression. It is a medical condition. My brain chemicals are not right." If this sounds like you or someone you know, please do not feel defensive, but continue reading. Although these statements might be accurate observations of medical science, they are not *who* God created you to be, and it will be very difficult for you to walk in healing and freedom as long as you claim these words by speaking them aloud and believing them in your heart. This creates an *agreement* in the spiritual realm that bonds you to your symptoms. You can find a prayer to break the curse of a diagnosis in Appendix 3 at the end of this book. Pray this prayer for yourself or your loved ones related to any label or diagnosis that has been spoken over you or them. And then, going forward, choose to speak life over yourself and others.

Please know that *all words* have spiritual *power*. Be very careful to never speak evil or deceit (as we are warned in today's verses), as it will lead to suffering in your life. One of the fruits of being a Spirit-filled Christian is that we have self-control. This means we must learn to speak differently than the world. When we hold back the words we think might be funny or emotionally satisfying, arguing in our mind that this person *deserves* them, we can then respond with a blessing instead. This is a *vital* Kingdom principle to learn and walk out in your daily life if you intend to have *"love and to see good days."* The spiritual law regarding the power in your words is so important that I would encourage you to study it and practice it with fervor in your life. I have several online resources, as well as my book, *It's Time for a Revolution,* that could aid in your deeper understanding of this mighty spiritual weapon. Your words truly contain the power of *life and death*.

Reflection

- In what ways have you used your words against yourself or others?
- Do you or a loved one have a diagnosis or perhaps just a label that you have received and now claim it as part of your identity? These can include things like: lazy, poor housekeeper, not good at reading, one who never has enough money, etc. These are all *word curses* that are not in alignment with what God says about you.
- What negative views of yourself or how the world sees you are causing you to believe and then speak negative words against yourself, your spouse, your family, or your children?
- Ask for forgiveness for these negative words and beliefs today, and then *daily* speak life, God's promises, and truth from His Word in order to contradict and replace those lies, training yourself to view your life through a Kingdom perspective. Watch as your mind, emotions, and body begin to heal. *Your words have power!*

DAY FOUR

The Kingdom Principle of Peace

To sum up, all of you be harmonious, sympathetic, loving, compassionate, and humble; not returning evil for evil or insult for insult, but giving a blessing instead; for you were called for the very purpose that you would inherit a blessing. For, "The one who desires life, to love and see good days, must keep his tongue from evil and his lips from speaking deceit. **He must turn away from evil and do good; he must seek peace and pursue it.** *For the eyes of the Lord are toward the righteous, and His ears attend to their prayer, but the face of the Lord is against evildoers"* (1 Peter 3:8–12 NASB).

Jesus brought a message of peace through His presence on earth. You will find, as you read Scripture through a Kingdom lens, that the gospel of Jesus is all about peace and love. Becoming a true Christ-follower gives you a sense of peace that no amount of material wealth or earthly relationships ever could. Jesus said, *"Peace I leave with you, My peace I give you; not as the world gives, do I give to you. Do not let your hearts be troubled, nor fearful"* (John 14:27 NASB).

The peace Jesus brings is supernatural. His message to believers is that we are to have peace in the most turbulent of life's storms, *knowing* we have a trustworthy Captain at the helm. Jesus slept in the same storm the disciples thought they would die in! Jesus rested in peace, trusting His Father in Heaven to keep them safe. When the doubting sailors (disciples) woke Him, Jesus spoke to the storm: *"Peace! Be still!"* (Mark 4:39 ESV). Some theologians believe Jesus was not necessarily speaking to the wind and the waves, but to the *peace* that He continually carried with Him. That peace exuded from His *very being* and then affected every atmosphere He entered. In the storm, He commanded this peace to manifest, and then *His* peace caused the storm to be stilled. Did you know you have this *same peace*? As believers, we are called to bring peace into every atmosphere and interaction through the Spirit of God living in us. Jesus told His disciples:

> *And whatever house you enter, first say, "Peace be to this house." And if a man of peace is there, your peace will rest upon him; but if not, it will return to you* (Luke 10:5–6 NASB).

Learning to give, release, and walk in supernatural peace brings an extraordinary comfort to every life situation we face. It is not your responsibility, nor is it within your control, to manage what other people *actually do* with the peace you bring, as this verse states. If they do not receive it or they are not changed by it, it will simply return to you.

Also, we are instructed in Ephesians 6 to put on the armor of God every day in order to protect our minds and emotions from the attacks of the enemy. Within these verses, we see that the warrior of Christ stays rooted in faith and truth by strapping on the sandals (or boots) of the gospel of *peace*. These are no ordinary shoes by the way; Paul was describing the dress of a Roman solider in biblical times. This special footwear had teeth, like cleats, so a solider in battle could stand firm, even while on unstable ground. This is the role Godly peace should play in the life of a believer. *"And the peace of God, which surpasses all comprehension, will guard your hearts and minds in Christ Jesus"* (Phil. 4:7 NASB).

Through the message of the gospel—God's everlasting love for us, secured by our relationship with Him through Christ—our minds and emotions can be steadied. No matter what our life circumstances might be, the biblical truth of God's peace will *ground us*. Having counseled many people through the worst imaginable life traumas, I have witnessed as they were sustained purely by their faith and found peace in situations that would baffle the rest of us. God's peace truly does surpass all understanding. Supernatural peace can be as real and palpable as a tangible hug from the Father Himself.

God values peace. It is the banner of His Kingdom here on earth. When the world experiences hunger, chaos, political uprising, disease, and death, the Church can be a rock and a safe place for those in need. The world looks to and needs those with steadfast faith in times of trouble. Though people may not know what it is that is so attractive about you, the peace of God will follow you wherever you go, and it will bring a light to every atmosphere you enter.

When a Christian exhibits peace and joy in unlikely life circumstances, it is one of the greatest testimonies of *who our God really is* to those who are not yet in relationship with Jesus. People take notice. From the counseling office to my personal home, people will often comment about how peaceful these places and atmospheres feel to them. It is a tangible experience, and it changes people when we share God's peace with them. It exists within our very *being,* and it will manifest everywhere we go, if you release it to do so. Do not underestimate the value of peace; it is a powerful fruit of your identity as a son or daughter of the one true Peacemaker. *"Blessed are the peacemakers, for they will be called sons* [and daughters] *of God"* (Matt 5:9 NASB).

Reflection

- What are the most difficult situations for you that seem to disrupt or steal your peace?
- How do you maintain a state of peace during fearful, stressful, or angering situations?
- In what ways do you need to improve in this area of your spiritual walk?
- Have you experienced the peace of God from either interaction with or observation of someone who demonstrates strong faith? What was it like, and how did it make you feel or inspire you?

DAY FIVE

The Effective Prayers of the Righteous

*To sum up, all of you be harmonious, sympathetic, loving, compassionate, and humble; not returning evil for evil or insult for insult, but giving a blessing instead; for you were called for the very purpose that you would inherit a blessing. For, "The one who desires life, to love and see good days, must keep his tongue from evil and his lips from speaking deceit. He must turn away from evil and do good; he must seek peace and pursue it. **For the eyes of the Lord are toward the righteous, and His ears attend to their prayer, but the face of the Lord is against evildoers**"* (1 Peter 3:8–12 NASB).

For many years, as a Christian counselor, I studied and pursued spiritual healing both for myself and for my clients. God planted a seed of passion for spiritual healing deep within me as part of my calling in His Kingdom. I have a lot of faith for supernatural signs, wonders, and healing through Christ, and I would never claim it was something I worked hard to have. Rather, it is a spiritual gift from the Father. I tell you all of this because, although I had great *faith in God* to perform miracles, it took me most of my adult life to learn how to be free of a *striving spirit*—trying to *make things happen* in life by my own efforts. Many times, my intentions were pure; with great faith I would push forward, and in the end, I would give God the glory for my positive outcome. Was I wrong to try so hard? Not necessarily, since faith without works is dead (see James 2:17 NASB).

But in regard to praying for people—laying hands on them to be healed mentally or emotionally, praying for their marriage or family to be reconciled, or teaching them to believe for a supernatural miracle in their bodies—because I did not always see the results I hoped for, I began to wonder whether certain Kingdom principles or spiritual keys could *lead to* prayers being answered more often than not.

The first answer to this question is that God is sovereign, and He heals whenever and whomever according to His divine will. But Scripture is also clear that living a Godly life, pursuing righteousness, and learning to think and act like Christ will enable you to be *more effective* in the Kingdom. If a believer walks in righteousness, it will only be because of an intimate and continuous connection to the Father. Only through our identity in Christ and constant recognition of our position as children of the Most High God can we *actually become* righteous. Outside of these two principles, everything else is fruitless human effort.

On my journey of breaking free from fleshly striving, the Holy Spirit taught me these three practical steps, which delivered me into *thriving in Christ*:

1. I must praise God for who He is so that I understand who I am.

I have learned that in order to fully rest in my identity in Christ and not slide back into striving, I needed to spend time worshiping and praising God for who He is. When I declared His authority, Kingship, and incredible love for me, I suddenly found it nearly impossible to question who He created *me* to be. I am His. I am destined for greatness because of Jesus. I was formed in my mother's womb with a destiny and purpose in His Kingdom. I did not achieve any of this by my own efforts. It is all because of who God is and what Jesus did on the cross for me. If that was not enough, He also sent His Spirit to reside on the inside of me, offering me guidance, leadership, and an on-going unveiling of His Kingdom revelation throughout my life here on earth. All this is to be used for His glory.

But if I forget to praise Him, I begin to lose my ground, my foundation, and I am far more susceptible to believing the lies of the enemy about who I am and whether God is good. Without praise, worldly circumstances can drive my fears and doubts to the surface. The first step in effective prayer is to be grateful and offer thanksgiving to God for who He is and all He has already done for you. For this very reason, my life verse is Philippians 4:6: *"Do not be anxious about anything, but in everything by prayer and pleading* **with thanksgiving** *let your requests be made known to God." (NASB)*

2. I must embrace humility and confess my sins to others.

> *Therefore, confess your sins to one another, and pray for one another so that you may be healed. A prayer of a righteous person, when it is brought about, can accomplish much* (James 5:16 NASB).

As this verse instructs, we are to confess our sins to one another and pray for one another so that we may be *healed*. In order to be effective in the Kingdom, we must seek to be humble and free from sin, declaring that our righteousness comes from the blood of Jesus. His sacrifice is applied to our sins and makes us holy before God. Through this declaration, we are spiritually equipped to walk in power and authority. I have found that the act of confession and giving and receiving forgiveness are the most effective spiritual tools to release *miraculous healing* in one's life.

3. I must pursue fellowship with other believers.

It is also very important and helpful to make these confessions to one another, as believers. Having true and vulnerable fellowship with our brothers and sisters in Christ holds us accountable. It enables us to be strong for each other during times when our brothers and sisters in Christ might be feeling weak, discouraged, or defeated. And it also gives us the opportunity to challenge one another, to ensure we are not being distracted or deceived, and to be vigilant in our quest for Godliness. When we make our confession and repentance solely a private matter, it is very easy for a spirit of pride to sneak its way in. The path to righteousness is a journey we are not meant to take alone. Although you will certainly encounter detours along this road, if you are armed with your spiritual weapons of **praise, confession,** and **fellowship,** you will be ushered back into a righteous and God-honoring lifestyle every time.

Reflection

- How does it make you feel to learn that God sees and hears the prayers of the righteous? Do you include yourself in that category? Why or Why not?
- Have you had the experience of recognizing *your heavenly position* through praising God *for who He is* first?
- How have you seen the act of confession play a role in your ability to walk in righteousness? Is this something you feel convicted about and perhaps need to do more of in your life? What about confessing to another person?
- Are you in fellowship with at least one person who holds you accountable, who holds you up in prayer, and who helps to meet your emotional needs? Does this person direct you back onto the path of truth and a God-honoring and righteous lifestyle?

Jessica Rothmeyer PhD

_____

_____

_____

_____

_____

_____

_____

_____

_____

_____

_____

_____

_____

_____

_____

_____

WEEK SIX

A Call to Righteousness

Who is there to harm you if you prove zealous for what is good? But even if you should suffer for the sake of righteousness, you are blessed. And do not fear their intimidation, and do not be in dread, but sanctify Christ as Lord in your hearts, always being ready to make a defense to everyone who asks you to give an account for the hope that is in you, but with gentleness and respect; and keep a good conscience so that in the thing in which you are slandered, those who disparage your good behavior in Christ will be put to shame (1 Peter 3:13–16 NASB).

We concluded last week by studying how God listens when a *righteous* person prays. This week we will spend five more days studying in depth how each Christian is *called to righteousness*. Through your relationship with Christ, you are supernaturally endowed with righteousness, which serves as a very important weapon in the spiritual arsenal you need in order to be victorious and walk in freedom in this life. Those who seek righteousness will endure persecution (some more than others), but Scripture offers a great deal of reassurance that God will be with you through it all. Any suffering you face for the sake of righteousness will be greatly rewarded.

DAY ONE

Finding Safety in Goodness

Who is there to harm you if you prove zealous for what is good? *But even if you should suffer for the sake of righteousness, you are blessed. And do not fear their intimidation, and do not be in dread, but sanctify Christ as Lord in your hearts, always being ready to make a defense to everyone who asks you to give an account for the hope that is in you, but with gentleness and respect; and keep a good conscience so that in the thing in which you are slandered, those who disparage your good behavior in Christ will be put to shame* (1 Peter 3:13–16 NASB).

One of the most comforting aspects of being a Christian is being protected by God's justice. He is full of mercy and grace, and His omniscient wisdom is far greater and more trustworthy than any judge or jury here on this earth. Knowing this, we can walk in confidence as believers. If we share in the heart and mind of Christ, God will protect us and will ensure righteous judgment for our enemies.

> *"No weapon that is formed against you will succeed; and you will condemn every tongue that accuses you in judgment. This is the heritage of the servants of the Lord, and their vindication is from Me," declares the Lord* (Isaiah 54:17 NASB).

Does this protection and justice from the Lord equate to a life without suffering, a life in which you are never falsely accused, rejected, or abused? No, that is not the case, as we have already learned in this study. What it does mean is that as we put our whole faith and trust in God and believe He is truly for us, the love of God and our salvation through Christ will see us through every attempt by the enemy to cause pain or destruction in our lives. As Paul wrote:

> *For I am convinced that neither death, nor life, nor angels, nor principalities, nor things present, nor things to come, nor powers, nor height, nor depth, nor any other created thing will be able to separate us from the love of God that is in Christ Jesus our Lord* (Romans 8:38–39 NASB).

This type of thinking is anti-intuitive. As humans, we want our own justice. When we are hurt, we are concerned with protecting ourselves or our loved ones, trying to ensure painful experiences never happen again. But that is not always Godly thinking. This type of worldly advice and self-preservation can often lead a person to act or speak in ways that are not righteous or holy. It is very difficult to sustain a clean heart, free of unforgiveness, if you take on the responsibility of procuring *your own* justice in life. Instead, through reading God's Word, you will come to believe and *trust* that God's justice is always better than your own. At times, He will be more merciful than you think someone *deserves*, but rest assured, He will also be more merciful with you than *you* deserve. We all need His mercy and grace more often than we think we do. At other times, your enemies or those who have hurt you will suffer consequences that will break your heart, as God might give you a glimpse into *His heart* and show you how the suffering of His children causes Him to grieve greatly.

In order to have peace in your mind and healing in your physical body, I encourage you to *labor into* His rest, trusting in God's goodness to protect and provide for you *every day*. This type of surrendered faith is the only way to live in victory this side of Heaven. Once you can let go of fear and your own self-effort to control or protect yourself and your family, then you will be released to focus on what truly brings peace and joy in life—spreading the gospel and demonstrating the love of Christ wherever you go. In the future, when you *do suffer* and experience an evil attack, respond like Jesus would: *"Do not be overcome by evil, but overcome evil with good"* (Rom. 12:21 NASB).

When you show love, care, mercy, and forgiveness to those who have come against you, when you praise God in the middle of a spiritual attack, when you declare God's promises in life's worst moments, God will protect you and deliver you with His perfect justice. You can count on it.

Reflection

- Journal or discuss a time when you have experienced injustice in your life. How did you handle it? What happened after that?
- If you struggle to trust God in dealing with your enemies and those who have hurt you, what would you like Him to do? Is your response biblical?
- Give some life examples of when you chose to do good in the midst of being hurt, offended, or betrayed? How did it make you feel? What happened in the end?
- Do you recognize how pleasing it is to the Lord when you choose to repay evil with good? Describe how you imagine your Father reacting to your Christ-like actions. What would He say to you? What would He do in return?

DAY TWO

Suffering Brings Change

Who is there to harm you if you prove zealous for what is good? **But even if you should suffer for the sake of righteousness, you are blessed.** *And do not fear their intimidation, and do not be in dread, but sanctify Christ as Lord in your hearts, always being ready to make a defense to everyone who asks you to give an account for the hope that is in you, but with gentleness and respect; and keep a good conscience so that in the thing in which you are slandered, those who disparage your good behavior in Christ will be put to shame* (1 Peter 3:13–16 NASB).

It did not take very long, as a mental health professional, for me to observe that the single most effective agent for change in people's lives is pain. Pain can cause a person to desire life change for issues that would otherwise have been ignored, emotionally stuffed, or dismissed. Whether it is a wife's threat of divorce that causes her husband to take his marriage seriously or a diagnosis of diabetes that finally convinces a distracted businessman to prioritize healthy eating—pain and suffering bring about change.

I cannot tell you how many times I have promised God, after a difficult season in my life, that I would never take Him or His grace for granted ever again—and then life happens. We become complacent or apathetic in ways we do not even notice. I would rationalize that I was still a good Christian: "I love Jesus. I pray every day. I read my Bible and go to church faithfully. I am generous in giving, and I try to always be kind to others." These are all valid and true statements in my life. But was I strengthening my faith? Was I pursuing God and His will for my life with a *burning* passion? Was my heart soft and breaking for what breaks His heart? Was I allowing myself to see or experience the true pain in me and in the world that motivates a person in ways that no amount of church ever can?

> *After you have suffered for a little while, the God of all grace, who called you to His eternal glory in Christ, will Himself perfect, confirm, strengthen, and establish you* (1 Peter 5:10 NASB).

I wish there was another way to keep people on the path to righteousness. But my many years as a mental health professional and spiritual mentor have proven that this biblical truth is accurate: Pain leads to change. Humans naturally revert to a state of pleasure, comfort, and self-preservation if left to their own instincts. Evil and suffering are orchestrated and influenced by Satan, but God *allows* us to experience it, because we live in a fallen world. One day when we go to Heaven, we will be reunited with the Father, and suffering of every kind will cease. But for now, Satan is the prince of this dark world, and as a result, disease, evil people, desperate circumstances, and heart-break bring us pain. But have hope! Jesus reassures us: *"...In the world you have tribulation, but take courage; I have overcome the world"* (John 16:33 NASB).

When we suffer for the sake of righteousness, knowing God is refining us in ways a lifestyle of comfort never could, we can trust that suffering like Christ suffered brings honor to God. And it builds a strength and hope in Jesus within us that we might not otherwise have. Pain and suffering in our lives remind us that God is our central anchor in the storms of life. This should be our mindset: We cannot live without His presence and love, which are a steadfast lifeline that carries us through the darkest of days. Jesus overcame sin on the cross and defeated death by His resurrection so that, no matter how hopeless life seems in the natural, our minds and hearts can find comfort in knowing we have a Savior. Our victory has already been won; the battle is short and meaningless compared to our lives in eternity.

Jesus will accompany you through the pain, and as you share in His sufferings, your faith will grow. Your awareness of God's tangible love for you will increase. And your righteousness will become more and more evident. With this Kingdom mindset, you can embrace and even rejoice in the suffering, knowing the outcome is for God's glory.

Reflection

- Think of some painful experiences that, with hindsight, you can see increased your faith and strengthened your trust in the Lord.
- How have you blamed God or been unforgiving of yourself or others *before* you had a Godly mindset about pain and suffering? How do you feel about it now?
- Can you see how pain is motivating? Give specific life examples.
- In what ways have you changed because of your personal sacrifice, knowing that suffering for righteousness' sake would be worth it in the end?

DAY THREE

Godly Confidence

*Who is there to harm you if you prove zealous for what is good? But even if you should suffer for the sake of righteousness, you are blessed. **And do not fear their intimidation, and do not be in dread, but sanctify Christ as Lord in your hearts,** always being ready to make a defense to everyone who asks you to give an account for the hope that is in you, but with gentleness and respect; and keep a good conscience so that in the thing in which you are slandered, those who disparage your good behavior in Christ will be put to shame* (1 Peter 3:13–16 NASB).

If you think about *truly suffering* for the sake of righteousness, being an ambassador of Christ, you have to know that others will try to intimidate you, persecute you, and belittle your faith. These acts of warfare against believers have been happening since biblical times. Before Paul truly knew Jesus, he claimed to be a Godly man, fighting for righteousness, while persecuting and even killing many Christians. After his conversion, Paul grieved his previous actions. These painful memories motivated Paul to be a bold and outspoken warrior for the Kingdom of God, for which he suffered with joy knowing that truth would overcome evil in the end.

With this kind of thinking and with a pure heart posture (with no self-ambition), Christians can walk in a Godly confidence that is mysterious to non-believers. As Paul and the other apostles began to spread the good news, the world witnessed signs, wonders, and miraculous healings in the name of Jesus. This made it very difficult for their critics to continue making their ugly or disbelieving comments. Many were converted, and the Church grew rapidly. The same will hold true for believers today. Those who have made Jesus their Savior and testify that the Bible is absolute truth can hold their heads high, even in the midst of accusation. What other *humans* think is of little concern. What God, His Word, and His Spirit bring into our lives is a kind of comfort and validation that is truly healing, freeing, and ever-present.

> *And now, Lord, look at their threats, and grant it to Your bond-servants to speak Your word with all confidence, while You extend Your hand to heal, and signs and wonders take place through the name of Your holy servant Jesus* (Acts 4:29–30 NASB).

In these verses, the disciples cry out for God to give them bold confidence to do His will and for God to reveal His goodness and glory through signs, healings, and wonders in the name of Jesus. When Peter wrote, in our verse for this week, *"And do not fear their intimidation, and do not be in dread,"* he was quoting from Isaiah 8:12. I find such beauty in the fabric of its truth. That Peter could quote from a passage written hundreds of years previous and have it apply to *their* circumstances at that time should give us great confidence in the Word of God. Isaiah's words comforted his contemporaries, yet they also became a statement of confidence and encouragement for the apostles, and now they bring wisdom to us and continue to direct our paths *today*, as modern-day holy women. The Word of God is truly timeless.

The confidence we receive from God in our spirits is something no amount of schooling, self-help books, or false arrogance could ever establish. The Spirit of God within each believer releases grace and truth in the moment we need it, and we can put our complete faith and trust in Him. Many times, some of the best counsel I have offered to wives, parents, and pastors was to rest in the goodness of God and His Word, rather than relying on their own efforts or human interventions. People are sometimes swayed to walk away from their Godly convictions because of trying to please the world or force an outcome that was not part of God's plan.

These verses tell us our trust must be in God, even when others try to intimidate or persuade us to align with their worldly perspective. Hold fast to the promises that God so poignantly communicates in His Word, and look to your testimony for reassurance. How has God shown His love, His healing power, and His faithfulness in your life? These testimonies are demonstrations of who He is and what your faith in Him can do. In times when you are tempted to feel troubled, never forget who you are in Christ and the righteousness and authority you *already have*. It's time to function as the holy and powerful citizen of Heaven that you are! Walk in bold confidence. Do not lose sight of the fact that Jesus has already overcome the world, including anyone who tries to come against you.

Reflection

- What conflicts, confrontations, or intimidating situations have you encountered in regard to sharing or living out your faith?
- What has been or is now your mindset in being confident that God will see you through your suffering?
- I encourage you to pray for boldness and courage to do God's will and to not be intimidated, ashamed, or persuaded into assimilating to a worldly culture. You are equipped, through His Spirit and His Word, to face suffering for righteousness' sake.

Jessica Rothmeyer PhD

_____

_____

_____

_____

_____

_____

_____

_____

_____

_____

_____

_____

_____

_____

_____

DAY FOUR

Self-control

*Who is there to harm you if you prove zealous for what is good? But even if you should suffer for the sake of righteousness, you are blessed. And do not fear their intimidation, and do not be in dread, but sanctify Christ as Lord in your hearts, **always being ready to make a defense to everyone who asks you to give an account for the hope that is in you, but with gentleness and respect;** and keep a good conscience so that in the thing in which you are slandered, those who disparage your good behavior in Christ will be put to shame* (1 Peter 3:13–16 NASB).

In order to live out our calling as *holy women*, as a holy nation of believers under God, we must activate this very important fruit of the Spirit: self-control. Whether we are being confronted or belittled, or someone is asking in sincere interest about our hope in Jesus, we must learn how to respond with gentleness and respect to the other person, seeing them as a creation of God and honoring *Him* by being controlled in our response, no matter how others treat us.

When I first read this verse, I thought about how easy it is to tell people about my faith when they ask things like: "Why are you so happy all the time?" "You seem so calm, even though I know your life is difficult right now. How can that be?" But as I counseled many non-believers and ministered to people in the community, I discovered that their questions and comments often were not very kind or *genuinely* inquisitive. Instead, they were full of sarcasm and disdain. Many people do not *know* God and have little comprehension of His truth found in Scripture; therefore, their ideas and assumptions and the offenses they hold against Him are based on false beliefs and deceptive worldly teachings. "If God is so great, why does He let bad things happen? I'm mad at God, because my parents died when I was young. My life is horrible; why doesn't He intervene? God doesn't care. I've tried praying many times, and He hasn't answered any of my requests. You just use your faith as a crutch, and you don't actually live in reality." I have heard all of these comments in response to my testimony of faith. But these comments are usually the overflow of great pain. Though they don't know it, these people are actually longing for a relationship with their Creator.

The Word tells us that if we are going to be salt and light to the world, representing Jesus well, our thoughts, words, and actions must go through a Kingdom filter. Love, mercy, grace, and forgiveness must be at the forefront of our minds as we give an answer or explanation to those who question our faith. *"A gentle answer turns away wrath, but a harsh word stirs up anger"* (Prov. 15:1 NASB).

> *Older men are to be temperate, dignified, self-controlled, sound in faith, in love, in perseverance. Older women likewise are to be reverent in their behavior, not malicious gossips nor enslaved to much wine, teaching what is good* (Titus 2:2–3 NASB).

It is so important for men and women of faith to respond to the world around them with love, *yet* also continue to teach what is right and noble. It is perhaps our greatest battle in this modern world: to stand by the absolute truth in God's Word, yet express it in a way that is loving and respectful, refusing to allow the reaction of non-believers to offend us or to cause an ungodly response of harsh words or rejecting behaviors. Even if you are loving and respectful, people might still mock you, reject you, or even threaten you. Preparing ourselves for this, we must not allow our fear or our desire to win over the world to water down what Scripture actually says.

Christians must be vigilant in knowing God's Word to protect themselves from making *any* agreements with the world's false or deceived views about a righteous lifestyle. Believers must stand firm and be careful not to *become* like those they are trying to minister to. This can be an emotional and even intellectual battle. Where does the line of love for others cross over into compromising God's perfect truth? This verse reminds us that we must not be intimidated into denying or modifying God's Word in order to appease others. Rather, we must do our best to represent Jesus and the Word *in love* while refusing to compromise our convictions, which is when suffering for righteousness' sake may happen.

Reflection

- How have you responded when you were asked why you believe what you do about Jesus?
- Have you ever been persecuted? Was it for standing up for the absolute truth found in God's Word?
- Pray that God will give you strength and the Holy Spirit will speak through you in times when you must suffer for righteousness' sake so that you may respond with Christ-like love and honor to any who challenge your faith.

DAY FIVE

God's Vengeance

Who is there to harm you if you prove zealous for what is good? But even if you should suffer for the sake of righteousness, you are blessed. And do not fear their intimidation, and do not be in dread, but sanctify Christ as Lord in your hearts, always being ready to make a defense to everyone who asks you to give an account for the hope that is in you, but with gentleness and respect; **and keep a good conscience so that in the thing in which you are slandered, those who disparage your good behavior in Christ will be put to shame** (1 Peter 3:13–16 NASB).

Yesterday we discussed the importance of responding to others with self-control, even if they are triggering us into an instinctual reaction of defensiveness. This is a natural human response when being attacked, accused, or questioned unjustly. Peter, the author of these words, fell victim to his flesh on the night Jesus was arrested in the garden. He drew his sword and sliced off the ear of one of the servants of those who were coming to take Jesus away (see John 18:10). Peter knew Jesus was innocent, and he was simply trying to come to His defense.

Like Peter, Christians try to justify their harsh reactions, claiming they are acting in defense of the gospel. But with spiritual maturity and the intervention of the Holy Spirit, Christ-followers are to respond in a way that is Christ-like, *not instinctual.* Trying to stuff your emotions or just white-knuckle it in the moment is not sustainable. You must be able to walk away from confrontational situations with complete peace of mind. If you continue to ruminate about it or have unresolved feelings about your negative interactions with others, you will not be able to walk in spiritual freedom.

Sometimes, this step is really, really hard! Some people might ask about or challenge your faith in a fairly diplomatic way. In those situations, you can easily respond with a kind answer. They may think about your response for a moment or two before dismissing it. They may even ask you more questions, opening their hearts to a few seeds of truth that you could sow. But many others, whether in person, via social media, or through worldly false teaching, will unapologetically attack and degrade biblical wisdom. As believers, we must continue to live in mental, emotional, and spiritual health, even in the midst of being slandered or hated for speaking God's truth or living a righteous lifestyle.

When handling and coping with these controversial situations, we must remember that *God is responsible* for the outcome. We can put our faith and trust in Him to balance the scales of justice in the end. Through our self-control and obedience, refusing to take the situation into our own hands (and invariably mucking it up), we are actually giving God His due power and authority. Here is a piece of spiritual advice that has radically changed my life and affected my overall mental and emotional well-being: Know that God sees *everything*. For those who come against His Word, His Son, and His family of believers, the Lord's vengeance is unlike anything we can imagine. You *do not* mess with God or His people. *"Never take your own revenge, beloved, but leave room for the wrath of God, for it is written: 'Vengeance is Mine, I will repay,' says the Lord"* (Rom. 12:19 NASB).

God will protect that which is true and just. As you grow in your faith and see Him work in your life, you will learn that you can trust in His justice system, especially in times when you surrender and do not try to orchestrate your own vengeance or prove that you have been wronged. Jesus' reward and justice came after He gave the ultimate sacrifice—His life. Then God's vengeance was complete, defeating sin and death for all eternity. So, it is with great wisdom and restraint that we must continue to respond in love and honor toward those who assail us so that God's full justice will come to fruition. And in the meantime, Scripture reassures us that God will protect us. *"In the mouth of the foolish is a rod for his back, but the lips of the wise will protect them"* (Prov. 14:3 NASB).

As we have previously discussed, it is so important that we, as Christians, use our words to bless, not curse. Those who slander you *will be held accountable.* If you allow the justice to come from God, then you can walk free of any guilt or regret, and it protects you from any spiritual bondage in the process. Remember, to suffer in ways similar to how Christ suffered is an *honor.* We can be assured that we are being refined and blessed, fulfilling our holy position just like the Godly men and women who came before us. They left a righteous and God-honoring legacy for future generations to live by, and *you* can be a part of that legacy.

> *Blessed are you when people insult you and persecute you, and falsely say all kinds of evil against you because of Me. Rejoice and be glad, for your reward in heaven is great; for in this same way they persecuted the prophets who were before you* (Matthew 5:11–2 NASB).

Reflection

- Do you have a specific example of someone slandering, lying about, insulting you, or talking about you behind your back? What happened when the truth came out? How did you handle that process?
- If this has happened to you, but truth and justice have not yet taken place, how do you feel about your unsettled situation?
- Do you trust that God will have His vengeance in the end?
- Journal and discuss the mindset you should have in difficult situations (based on this week's study)—restraining yourself from giving a verbal rebuttal, yet walking away with peace, fully releasing it to the Lord.

WEEK SEVEN

Suffering for the Sake of Righteousness

For it is better, if God should will it so, that you suffer for doing what is right rather than for doing what is wrong (1 Peter 3:17 NASB).

You might be thinking, "Are we really spending an entire week on suffering for the sake of righteousness? Haven't we discussed this topic enough already?" As a counselor, I have discovered the *life-changing* value in teaching people about suffering. Suffering is a natural and necessary experience in life. Convincing both men and women, young and old, that suffering for righteousness' sake is part of our spiritual journey has been one of the most difficult challenges in my career. In America, most people are upset if they have to feel uncomfortable for even a second, let alone *suffer*. Why would a person suffer willingly? The only motivation I have found for enduring suffering is a love and passion for Christ. After you experience His unconditional and selfless love, it is a natural human reaction to want to offer it in return. If you are currently not compelled to do this, it helps to spend some alone time worshipping Father God, soaking in His presence. Worship reminds us of how good His love and grace are and just how much we need Him every day. For this eternal love, one would suffer. I pray that spending five days on this single verse deepens your passion for Christ and inspires you to suffer for righteousness' sake in your journey toward becoming a modern-day holy woman.

DAY ONE

The Perfect Parent

For it is better, if God should will it so, *that you suffer for doing what is right rather than for doing what is wrong* (1 Peter 3:17 NASB).

For the first five years of my counseling career, I facilitated in-home family therapy. A significant part of my job was to educate families on healthy boundaries, model appropriate parent-child interactions, and teach them parenting skills. For many of these parents, the only knowledge they had in the area of parenting was from their own childhood. Therefore, it was common to see dysfunctional and even abusive behaviors passed down from generation to generation. I begin today's study with this scenario, because it is in the most basic of human psychology that people project *onto God* what they have experienced within their *human* relationships. If you experienced a parent who was not very loving or protective, someone who left you feeling alone or neglected, that can affect your perception of who your Father in Heaven is and how you relate to Him. If you had a spouse who left you, saying they no longer loved you, do you believe God could also stop loving you and will abandon you?

Teaching people the character of God is vital in helping them step into a Kingdom mindset. Such a mindset enables them to see, hear, relate to, and respond to God in *truth*, not based on their unhealthy life experiences. The only way to ensure that our perception of God's attributes is accurate is to read about them in Scripture and to put our faith in *those words* as the iron-clad promises made by an infallible Father. Then, we must open ourselves to experiencing the saving grace of the one true Savior, which will cement His *true nature* into our hearts and minds forever. One of the most basic and crucial truths we need to know about God is that He is the *perfect parent.*

> *"For I know the plans that I have for you," declares the Lord,*
> *"plans for prosperity and not for disaster, to give you a future*
> *and a hope"* (Jeremiah 29:11 NASB).

Many of us have seen this verse before, written on the inside of graduation cards or displayed on a crafted sign we hang in our homes, but do we sincerely and whole-heartedly believe these words to be true? Do you believe God has only good intentions for you and your life, that you can put your hope and trust in Him and His will for your life? Like a healthy parent in the natural, God knows what we need better than we can know or choose for ourselves. Loving parents only want what is best for their children, and if children listen to their advice and trust their parents, their lives will be better for it. Children can be spared many poor decisions and suffering by listening to the wise counsel of their parents.

But often, it is not until they touch the hot stove, are rejected by their first love, or have an empty gas tank (because they spent their money unwisely) that children experience the *pain* that then helps them make different choices. Suffering brings about change. Unfortunately, many modern parents rescue their children from experiencing any suffering, and it has produced a generation of young adults who have no coping skills, who are experiencing increased mental health diagnoses, and who constantly complain of physical ailments that keep them from fully functioning. Many declare they are unable to work a steady or self-sustaining job due to their many issues. Modern parenting can often be dismissive; parents are either busy with their own careers, working two jobs in order to provide, or have recently divorced and are now dating, being distracted with a new love interest rather than spending time with their children. A lack of interaction and quality time from a parent automatically gives permission to the world to educate and (poorly) raise their children. This is a very dangerous and ungodly pattern we have allowed to happen for several generations now, and it is *evident* in the behaviors, mindsets, and overall life outcomes in our world today.

But this is not who our God is. He is loving, protective, and has a very specific plan and destiny for every life, which includes every person having a significant and lasting effect on the world around them. No life is meant to be spent in misery or focused on "self". By choosing a Godly path and living a righteous lifestyle, you will invite suffering, but also *prosperity*. Sometimes your suffering will be mildly uncomfortable and will motivate you or redirect you back onto a Godly path, and at other times, it will be a more drastic change that is needed to get your attention, refining you to be more and more like Christ.

God is good. He is not *causing* the suffering in your life. That is *always* from the evil realm or your own flesh. Whether it is another human hurting you, your own self-destructive thoughts and behaviors, or a *direct attack* from Satan, pain and suffering is never from God. But He will allow it. Just like the child who touches the hot stove, sometimes we need to experience the *ungodly* first in order to embrace the Godly, the *true nature* of our Father in Heaven. As our verse for this week instructs, we will experience suffering in this life, *"if God should will it,"* and we can trust it will be for our good and His glory!

Reflection

- How do you view the attributes and characteristics of Father God? Has it changed over time, as you learn more about Him through reading the Word and experiencing His love and grace in your life?
- Or do you struggle to believe He is for you, that His intentions are still good in the midst of suffering? Do you tend to blame God for your difficult life circumstances? Give examples.
- How have your parenting style, advice, and reactions to your children's misbehavior changed as you learned the true nature of your Father in Heaven? Has your mindset on that changed through this study?

DAY TWO

A Comfort Addiction

For it is better, if God should will it so, **that you suffer** *for doing what is right rather than for doing what is wrong* (1 Peter 3:17 NASB).

Suffering is a bizarre concept that is mostly avoided in sermons and church forums today. Is it truly part of God's will for us to experience pain and suffer? I wonder whether the lack of biblical teaching on this is the reason so many people question God's goodness and eventually blame Him for the misery in their lives. As we have discussed, the way the Kingdom of God operates is *very different* from our modern views. God is *always* good. Most often, we cause the suffering we experience through a lack of biblical wisdom. Most people are truly their own worst enemy.

The fact that suffering is part of our faith walk is a Kingdom principle that has been watered down or completely left out of most modern Christian teaching. The fact is, suffering is just a part of life on earth. For thousands of years, since the Fall in the garden of Eden, people have endured greater suffering than anything we experience today. The generations before us experienced famines and droughts that lasted years. Women and children frequently died during childbirth. Wars, devastating plagues, and epidemics claimed millions of lives. Throughout most of history, people frequently died because of harsh weather conditions, starvation, and unknown sicknesses. But in our modern world, especially in first-world countries, we are accustomed to every creature comfort money can buy, and then some!

As we discussed earlier, outward beauty can become an idol that causes devastating effects to one's mental, emotional, and physical health. I believe the idol of *comfort* has very similar repercussions. All of the first-world nations of today are addicted to comfort. With all the advancements in medicine and technology, it seems there is little the experts of this world cannot provide to meet society's demand for constant comfort. Do you have a headache? There's a pill for that. Do you need someone to shop and deliver your groceries? There is a service for that. Do you need next-day delivery so you can have a new TV by the weekend for the big game? There's an app for that. Do you need to pass time while waiting for an appointment? Your phone has a newsfeed or video to keep you and your kids entertained.

I often think about how the generations before us lived, about how difficult basic daily survival was for them. Then, as I listen to the complaints of my counseling clients about life circumstances that would have been considered so minor to our ancestors, I think, "What a bunch of spoiled babies we (me included) have become!" Someone's day is ruined if their Wi-Fi goes down. People have mental and emotional breakdowns (literally) if they have to wait more than a few minutes in a checkout line at a retail store. And the smallest level of rejection causes individuals to threaten suicide and require medical intervention. I wish I were exaggerating, but these are all real-life scenarios I hear, daily, in the counseling office and within my social circles.

Common areas of comfort addiction include the need for physical comfort, zero pain tolerance, an obsession with planning and organizing, a need-to-know mentality, control issues, ominous anxiety, daily mental stress due to high standards, a lack of endurance, a desire to prevent *all levels* of discomfort, and an insatiable hunger to experience contentment. Some people have all-out OCD (obsessive compulsive disorder) or panic disorders in attempts to avoid any type of pain or suffering. Many people today are living with the *overwhelming fear* of something they have *never experienced* and probably never will.

It doesn't help that our modern world has marketed every type of remedy to help in soothing these ungodly, fleshly desires. From a prescription medication for every kind of ache, pain, or mental and emotional issue there is, to things like retail therapy, online shopping, alcoholic beverages, drugs, secular music, sex addiction, and a variety of unhealthy coping mechanisms—we have been programmed to believe we should never have to endure pain. These empty promises of pain relief never last. They are simply distractions, trying to take the place of the one true Comforter.

The scariest part of this conditioning is that it has happened slowly over the course of several generations. Most people now have a worldly mindset in regard to suffering, (including Christians), which is: We should never have to suffer, *ever*. To them, suffering is an injustice, and they believe they should rage against and reject the idea of accepting a life with *even a hint* of pain or discomfort. This mentality says, "I don't deserve to feel this way! What did I ever do? This isn't right. My life is horrible. This isn't fair." You get the point. I'm sure you have heard and even personally said these phrases during times of frustration or challenging circumstances. Did you know this *ungodly mindset* can cause its own list of mental health issues and physical diseases?

Avoidance of physical or emotional pain is the leading cause of addictive behaviors. Initially, someone might be looking to ease their pain for a moment, but after experiencing the illusion of a time and space with no pain—perhaps feeling a momentary bliss while high, drunk, or swiping a credit card—this fleeting euphoria plants a root of addiction that is very hard to remove. When the pain returns (and it always does, usually with a vengeance), people begin to use more, spend more, and avoid and deny more in hopes that they never have to suffer or feel that pain again.

What if, instead, we *taught* our young people and *retrained* the older generations that pain and suffering are normal and serve a spiritual purpose in our lives? What if the normal, everyday assumption of the human race was that we will experience some level of pain and suffering in life, but it is not something to become anxious or depressed about? This *is* the message of the gospel. Jesus *suffered* for your sake so that you could live a life of freedom here on earth and enjoy life everlasting with Him in Heaven. Godly strengths and righteous characteristics are *born* out of pain and suffering. Being able to endure that pain gives one the courage to handle the difficult times in life.

Becoming a Christian and learning to walk with God does not protect you from suffering. But you will indeed have peace, joy, hope, and a promise of victory in the end because of Jesus. Certain aspects of our refinement and spiritual strengthening simply cannot happen without the worldly, human condition of pain and suffering. But do not be afraid. You can do it! *"I can do all things through Him who strengthens me"* (Phil. 4:13).

Reflection

- What specific types of pain and suffering do you try to avoid or medicate? What types cause you to be afraid?
- Can you see how the worldly desire to avoid pain has a devastating effect on our current society? In what ways?
- Can you reflect and journal about how the painful times in your life have changed you, deepened your faith, or improved your overall outlook on life?
- How would you explain this subject to others in order to help them break free of an addiction to needing *constant comfort*?

DAY THREE

Christian Superheroes

*For it is better, if God should will it so, **that you suffer for doing what is right** rather than for doing what is wrong* (1 Peter 3:17 NASB).

Thus far we have established that suffering will happen whether you try to avoid it or not, so if you must suffer, it might as well be for good. Plenty of people in the world, especially ones I described in yesterday's study, are trapped in addictions. Such people are deceived by false teaching and evil temptations and choose to do what is *wrong* in hopes of avoiding suffering. This only leads them down a path of *greater suffering*, forcing them to make poor choices over and over while caught in a self-defeating cycle of pain and avoidance. This type of suffering is awful. The *even greater* suffering, though, is in the *eternal consequences* of this behavior, which causes them to harden their hearts toward God and choose a life apart from Him.

On the flip side are those who choose the narrow path—following God whole-heartedly and willingly suffering for what is right. These wonderful souls are the *Christian superheroes* in our faith history. We can read the list of biblical greats in Hebrews 11, also known as the *Faith Hall of Fame*. From Abraham to Moses to David, we remember and honor them for their sacrifices and for the legacy of faith they left for all of us to continue to learn from, even today. Throughout history, incredible men and women of the faith have stood up for the weak, the innocent, the voiceless, and the poor; they have suffered and sacrificed for the good of others. As born-again believers, we must be willing to be rejected and ridiculed, and we must avoid people-pleasing in ungodly ways, even with our own family and friends. Suffering can be mental, emotional, or physical, but regardless of the form, in the end, we know it was for the good of others, for God's glory, and for the advancement of His Kingdom.

I believe missionaries are some of the most incredible modern-day Christian superheroes. They leave the comfort of their homes and their country, often feeling alone in a place where the culture may be very different and they may not even understand the language. What a sacrifice! What bravery they show in surrendering their lives in hopes of bringing the love of Christ and eternal salvation to those in foreign lands. Pastors and teachers of God's Word are also superheroes in my book. What a challenge and life-long mission it is to shepherd and lead people to God, to guide them to salvation, and then to educate and encourage the flock for the rest of their lives. Most church leaders experience very little reward and must often endure great attacks and daily battles due to their chosen ministry. Often the families of pastors suffer just as greatly. Though they may not be as enthusiastic about the vision, because they are not part of the daily interactions that inspire further sacrifice, they experience pain and suffering for the benefit and growth of God's church.

Another category of modern-day superheroes is the Christian who is married to a spouse who is not yet walking with the Lord. They sacrifice on a daily basis, as they live with someone they love and to whom they are bonded emotionally and spiritually, yet must watch this person continue to be *lost* as they lack a personal relationship with Jesus. Also included in this category are parents of teen and adult children who have walked away from the faith in which their parents raised them. These faithful and praying parents must watch as their beloved child suffers, struggling and floundering in a world of lies and deception, yet unwilling to take Godly wisdom or advice from the people who love them the most. If you fall into either of these two categories, please know that your suffering, your prayers of intercession, and your loving acts are *extremely* pleasing to God, and they *will* bear fruit.

Finally, the greatest of all Christian superheroes are martyrs. All of the disciples were killed because of their faith, with the exception of John. Throughout history, many have died for the name of Jesus, refusing to deny Him. Many Christians are being killed throughout the world today, more than we realize. They understand the honor of the ultimate sacrifice of dying for the One who gave us eternal life. When we put the act of martyrdom into Godly perspective, we should all feel convicted about complaining due to a boring sermon or mediocre worship music during a church service. In many parts of the world, people are *dying* for the love of their Savior. Being willing to suffer and "die" (literally or metaphorically-dying to self) for that which is good, righteous, and holy is the calling of every believer. If we take the time to reflect, we will recognize there are many Christian superheroes actively *making a difference* in the lives of others. Are you one of them?

Reflection

- Who is your favorite Christian superhero? Choose someone from Scripture or from more recent times. It could even be a friend, a mentor, or a parent.
- Would you include yourself in this category? How might you be deemed a Christian superhero, suffering for that which is good?
- How do non-believers suffer in ways that do not bring about change and are not for the good of themselves or others? What do you observe about their mindsets and worldly beliefs that keeps them stuck in their unrighteous lifestyles?

DAY FOUR

The Worldly Path

*For it is better, if God should will it so, that you suffer for doing what is right **rather than for doing what is wrong*** (1 Peter 3:17 NASB).

Yesterday, one of the reflection questions asked for your observations of people who have worldly or ungodly mindsets. It becomes evident, as you study Scripture and gain wisdom about God's Kingdom, that little joy exists by living in and agreeing with the world. I could write a book (perhaps someday) about the parallel or correlating worldly beliefs, lies, and deceptions produced by the evil realm compared to the truth found in God's Word. I would then explain the direct outcomes, fruit, and life satisfaction that manifests from each of those mindsets.

Today's study is about those who choose to do what it wrong and follow the desires of their human flesh and how this path also leads to suffering. If suffering in this life is inevitable, we would be smart to choose to suffer for good, not evil. Unfortunately, the majority of people will not choose the narrow path to righteousness. Most of the population follows the worldly detour and succumbs to momentary pleasure and self-gratification, which will eventually result in their demise.

One major way Satan tempts people into choosing the wrong path is through an inner longing to be *like the world*. I believe this desire has really increased in its intensity with the introduction of social media. People long to be literally "liked" *by the world*, to be popular, and to look like those who are famous. Many people actually gain their followers by being exalted for rebellion against biblical or moral lifestyles. It can seem, in these modern circumstances, that these individuals believe they are on the right path because of the affirmation and encouragement they receive from the world. But Scripture warns us that we cannot simultaneously love the world and love God.

> *You adulteresses, do you not know that friendship with the world is hostility toward God? Therefore whoever wants to be a friend of the world makes himself an enemy of God* (James 4:4 NASB).

> *Do not love the world nor the things in the world. If anyone loves the world, the love of the Father is not in him. For all that is in the world, the lust of the flesh and the lust of the eyes and the boastful pride of life, is not from the Father, but is from the world* (1 John 2:15–16 NASB).

Let's break down the three main points in 1 John 2:15–16. If you choose the world over God, you will be overcome by the lust of the flesh, the lust of the eyes, and the boastful pride of life. As a professional counselor, I would create treatment plans and goals for my clients in the first few sessions. Over time, it became evident that *every issue* that caused suffering in their lives fell into one of these three categories.

The lust of the flesh describes how our carnal, human body has a mind of its own. Because we have a sinful nature, especially before we are saved and redeemed by Jesus, our flesh is constantly longing for gratification. If it is hungry, it wants to eat for strength and energy. Even if it is not hungry, it wants to eat for pleasure or comfort. If the flesh is cold, it wants warmth. If it has sexual desires, it seeks to be satisfied. Without strong conviction and a commitment to a holy lifestyle, many people, including Christians, fall to the lusts of the flesh. As many of us have experienced, giving into the lusts of the flesh *seldom* brings joy or comfort, and if it does, it will not last. Before long, the flesh will long for *more*.

The lust of the eye has to do with what we see and believe we should have, that which looks good and pleasing. Perhaps you long to have that perfectly decorated home, or you are jealous of the talents you see in someone who is successful. Maybe you are competitive, and you covet the physical appearance of the latest social media star. The compulsion to see other people as smarter, happier, prettier, or more successful causes many people a great deal of suffering in their lives. I have heard thousands of life stories in my career, and no one is, or ever will be, happy or content with their life *because of their worldly accomplishments, material possessions, or outward appearance.* No one.

The final temptation is the pride of life. God opposes the proud, and pride goes before a fall. We have all heard these biblical phrases, yet it is easy to be caught up in prideful thinking, speech, and behavior. Pride is not always boastful or arrogant; often it is disguised as false humility or martyrdom. Whether the person is tooting their own self-focused-horn, expressing bitterness for all they have had to sacrifice for others, or fishing for a compliment by complaining that they are never appreciated for their efforts, all of these mindsets come from of a spirit of pride and lead to bondage. The first step in avoiding a spirit of pride is to completely surrender your life to the will of God and lordship of Christ Jesus. If you try to hold onto and control even a single life goal or earthly desire, you will fall to the sin of pride. And it will create pain and suffering in your life.

Beware of these three areas of sin, which can so easily lead a person down an ungodly path, causing someone to suffer for doing what is *wrong.* No level of perfection is possible for us this side of Heaven. Only Jesus lived without sin. But when you recognize that you are going astray due to the diversions of the lust of the flesh, the lust of the eye, or the pride of life, simply repent, ask for forgiveness, and set your sights on the road that leads to righteousness once again.

Reflection

- Journal or discuss the ways you have fallen prey to the seduction of this world and how those choices brought suffering rather than satisfaction to your life.
- In what specific ways do you struggle with the lust of the flesh, the lust of the eye, or the pride of life?

- Please take time to reflect on the ways the Holy Spirit may be convicting you. Is He inviting you to enter into fuller surrender in certain areas of your life? To surrender your self-efforts, your accomplishments, or your future goals? Be encouraged. In exchange, you'll receive the perfect will of God for your life. This trust-fall will always lead you to healing and freedom. Do not skip this surrender step. In fact, repeat it often in order to walk in holiness and righteousness, which is the only path worthy of your suffering.

DAY FIVE

Having a Kingdom Mindset

For it is better, if God should will it so, that you suffer for doing what is right rather than for doing what is wrong (1 Peter 3:17 NASB).

When God called me out of individual counseling and transitioned me into doing more writing and speaking events, I felt like my ministry needed a new name. My counseling business was called *Divine Revelations*. This name emphasized that in every session I would assist my clients in asking *God* for the answers to their healing, knowing true freedom always comes through Christ, not by my efforts or advice. As I began to brainstorm and pray about this new branding, God reminded me of all the life experiences He had brought me through—from my own emotional issues as a teenager to my twenty years of clinical and spiritual case studies. The Holy Spirit very clearly communicated that I was to focus my teachings on how believers of today are to reject their worldly thinking and *return* to a *Kingdom Mindset*. This became the name of my new ministry. In my time as a counselor, I observed over and over that true and lasting healing came from aligning one's mind with Christ's and learning how the Kingdom of God operates.

In studying and applying the words of today's verse, it is important to have Godly thinking and to view life through a *Kingdom* lens. This means asking how your thought-life, emotions, and behaviors align with Scripture in order to live out God's will for your life. We have spent several days of this study learning about the spiritual growth that suffering can produce and how to tolerate our pain by likening our suffering to that of Jesus' life here on earth. For today's lesson, we will look at how to actually have joy in the suffering! Joy and suffering do not seem like they should be in the same sentence. They are antonyms by the world's standards, but their coexistence is a Kingdom principle all the same.

First, let's look to the disciples for our example. Peter and the apostles were arrested by the high priest and brought before the Council for preaching the gospel. They were almost executed, but due to God's protection, they were only beaten and then released. This was their response: *"So, they went on their way from the presence of the Council, rejoicing that they had been considered worthy to suffer shame for His name"* (Acts 5:41 NASB).

They *rejoiced*. I'm usually up for a good spiritual challenge, but this was intense! They endured ridicule, were called heretics, were threatened with death for continuing to preach, and were physically beaten. And *then* they left that situation rejoicing. It is hard for me to imagine having this same response. I clearly still have room for growth in this area. Through the deepening and maturing of my faith, I have come to realize that in order to *truly* align my mind, heart, and *whole being* to the Kingdom's order, I *must decisively choose* to find joy in my suffering.

As someone who has studied psychology for many years, I know this to be true: How you think, the lens you choose (and yes, you do have a choice) for viewing the world, your relationships, and your life struggles, will inevitably lead you down the path of your destiny. Many people are distracted and deceived by worldly teachings and false promises, and they are oppressed by unforgiveness and emotional wounds. All of these lead people into unhealthy choices. This type of suffering does not produce good fruit in life, nor does it bring glory to God. A lens, filter, or perspective that is not Godly will produce a life of misery. And because the human mind is fickle, easily influenced, and always changing, one must be steadfast in knowing and declaring God's Word in order to stay healthy and avoid being *constantly* deceived by the enemy.

That is why Scripture instructs us to *renew* our minds by reading God's Word. Because we live in a fallen world, our sin nature will rise up within us from time to time. We are in a battle every day in the spiritual realm. We must fight to stand firm in biblical truth, not allowing ourselves to be defeated by the lies of the dark forces that are warring against us, vying for our souls. No matter how long you have been a Jesus-follower, no matter the depth of your biblical knowledge, the effects of the evil realm are relentless and vicious, and in a moment, you can be encapsulated in a fog of deception, dread, and disbelief. But then, by reading one line of God's Word, the chains can fall off, light and truth can return, and your mind can see and think clearly again. That is why we need to *study the Bible*. We don't do it to be seen as holy by others, for religious reasons, or to fulfill a check on a spiritual to-do list; we read the Word for survival. To experience victory in life, we must hold onto God's truth, choosing to align with Kingdom principles every moment of our lives here on earth.

When you come to understand the role of suffering in your spiritual walk, you will see glimmers of hope in finding reasons to rejoice, just like the apostles did. You are walking in the shoes of Jesus by doing so. Your suffering could be executing a divine order to set future generations free from bondage. God might be strengthening your faith and your trust "muscles" for an exceptional breakthrough for His Kingdom. You will also be establishing more authority and Godly confidence in the spiritual realm with every life struggle you overcome. Suffering might be the only way to bring about the healing and life change that God intends for you, bringing you into your Kingdom destiny. There are many reasons for suffering, none of which *the world* understands or has a worthy explanation for. So, trust in God's promises and the instructions in His Word. Rejoice in your suffering for righteousness' sake, for *it will* bring glory to the Father and change you forever. You can find a list of Bible verses that speak to finding joy in times of suffering in Appendix 4 at the end of this book. Use these verses for meditation and encouragement during times of trouble. (John 16:33)

Reflection

- Journal or discuss a time when you have experienced joy in the midst of suffering. How did you come to feel that way? If that has not been your experience yet, describe how you tend to respond to difficult life situations?

- When the apostles rejoiced for suffering in Jesus' name, how do you think they came to those feelings and behaviors? What was *their mindset* at the time? How did they come to think this way?
- Do you have a testimony of going through a very difficult life circumstance and later realizing it was a spiritual battle? What kind of victory came out of this experience? Can you acknowledge you were strengthened in your faith and trust in the Lord? Did anything else of significance come out of this life struggle and pain?

WEEK EIGHT

Eternal Glory

For Christ also suffered for sins once for all time, the just for the unjust, so that He might bring us to God, having been put to death in the flesh, but made alive in the spirit; in which He also went and made proclamation to the spirits in prison, who once were disobedient when the patience of God kept waiting in the days of Noah, during the construction of the ark, in which a few, that is, eight persons, were brought safely through the water. Corresponding to that, baptism now saves you—not the removal of dirt from the flesh, but an appeal to God for a good conscience—through the resurrection of Jesus Christ, who is at the right hand of God, having gone into heaven, after angels and authorities and powers had been subjected to Him (1 Peter 3:18–22 NASB).

As we close with our final week of study, these verses describe a glorious ending, the victory Christ won for us at the cross and how to view our lives through *His* perspective—with an anticipation and knowledge of the eternal glory to come. This type of eternity-based mindset will lead you to many mental, emotional, and spiritual triumphs in life if you can keep ahold of it. The spiritual weapons that will ensure Kingdom advancements are: studying the Word, believing and declaring its truth, walking in your identity in Christ, having fellowship with like-minded believers, and nurturing a relationship with the Holy Spirit. God gave us an incredible, spiritual arsenal, but we must be aware, alert, and agile in our ability to use these weapons properly. Just as with any skill, we must put them into practice in order to experience any growth or benefit from them. It's time for war.

DAY ONE

Justified

For Christ also suffered for sins once for all time, the just for the unjust, so that He might bring us to God, *having been put to death in the flesh, but made alive in the spirit; in which He also went and made proclamation to the spirits in prison, who once were disobedient when the patience of God kept waiting in the days of Noah, during the construction of the ark, in which a few, that is, eight persons, were brought safely through the water. Corresponding to that, baptism now saves you—not the removal of dirt from the flesh, but an appeal to God for a good conscience—through the resurrection of Jesus Christ, who is at the right hand of God, having gone into heaven, after angels and authorities and powers had been subjected to Him* (1 Peter 3:18–22 NASB).

In my career, I spent a great deal of time studying the human persona and what types of traumas, abuse, and childhood wounds change and shape the way a person thinks and behaves. Then, God led me to the spiritual solution to healing: to live our lives from a Kingdom perspective. One of the most common indicators of someone who is really struggling in their mind and in their spirituality is someone who is easily offended. This reaction tells me this person is so wounded and insecure about their identity that they instinctually fight the world around them. They do this *because of* their unstable view of who they are, which comes from the lies they believe and unforgiveness within their souls. That sounds like a lot to comprehend, so let's unpack it a little.

Today's verse indicates that Jesus was the just One who died for the unjust (us). He was the perfect and spotless Lamb who was sacrificed to atone for the sins of the world. Anyone who puts their faith in Him will receive forgiveness and walk in His righteousness. A Christian is only holy and right before God in the courts of Heaven *because of Jesus*. Your good intentions and charitable deeds will never earn you a spot in eternity. *Never.* That is why Jesus had to die. Why would the Father allow His Son to suffer such a horrific death if it was not for an eternity-based reason?

With that being said, as a born-again believer, you are *now justified* before God, the Judge of the universe, and when He looks at you, all He sees is the Jesus in you. But is that how you see yourself? How can you live out your God-given role in His Kingdom if you are busy being offended and defensive over an identity that is *no longer you*? Perhaps you have already received this essential revelation, but if not, please know that you have been made pure. *You are holy.* You are the righteousness of God through Christ Jesus (see Rom. 3:22). You *were* unjust, unholy, and unworthy before God because of sin—until you took on the whole identity of Christ by putting your faith in Him as your Savior. In this way, you became a new creation, one that is now *just*. *"Therefore if anyone is in Christ, this person is a new creation; the old things passed away; behold, new things have come"* (2 Cor. 5:17 NASB).

It is essential to meditate *daily* on our Kingdom-based identity in order to experience mental and spiritual freedom, as well as to protect ourselves from future spiritual attacks. Satan has studied human nature since the beginning of time, and he will always attack you in the weakest chink of your armor (your identity). Because he is called the enemy, the devil is crafty in using the spiritual laws he understands (all too well) to hit people where it will hurt them the most. He accuses, shames, and guilts them for their sinful or ungodly words, thoughts, feelings, and actions. Because he knows *our spirits* already recognize that we have sinned (sometimes in the smallest of ways), he then orders his evil army to come and amplify those negative thoughts and feelings of shame or guilt, manifesting into a spirit of offense, which then causes us to act out by attacking others or becoming extremely defensive. The evil realm is very skilled in causing a ripple effect of hurt and pain that can exponentially affect many other people with one fell swoop, even future generations.

But Jesus justified God's people to such an extent that no lie, accusation, or sin allegation against them can ever stand up in Heaven's Court of Law. This spiritual gift is such an unbelievable reality! Many faith-filled Christians have never understood its full implications. No matter what you have done or will do in your lifetime, Jesus paid the price for it *already*. You are fully justified, and nothing you could say or do will be able to fulfill your debt without God's spiritual acquittal. The question is: How will you remind yourself of this valuable and priceless sacrifice made on your behalf? Meditating on it will enable you to resist being offended, reacting defensively, or attacking others in times of spiritual warfare.

I have coached, counseled, and walked this journey many times with hundreds of clients; when you accept the full justification of Jesus, taking on His identity as righteous and holy, you will experience healing in your mind, emotions, and within your physical body. Imagine if you could truly walk in this Christ-based justification. When someone (including yourself) accuses you of not being good enough in some way, you will no longer feel wounded or unleash an attack in return. You can stand firm in the knowledge that you have *already been justified* before God; therefore, no person can condemn you, and your only response needs to be one of grace and love. This is exactly how God responds to you, because of the righteousness you have in Christ.

I have found that the best way to stay grounded in a Christ-based identity is to declare Scripture. Declarations help to retrain your mind (and your whole soul) to be positioned to live from a Kingdom perspective. You will find a list of Christ-based identity verses in Appendix 2 at the end of this book. I suggest picking one verse to declare and memorize every day. Speak them over your life, your spouse's life, and the lives of your children. This is our only hope in standing firm in our faith and increasing our success rate in the battles against the enemy. Victory is ours, Christian soldiers! Let us never forget we are justified by our righteousness in Christ.

Reflection

- What are some of the chinks in your armor? In what ways are you easily triggered into becoming defensive or internalizing people's accusations or judgments against you?
- Journal and discuss how God sees and responds to your sin compared to *how the world* does. Can you identify how this revelation could set you free in your mind and affect your overall behaviors in life?
- How have you tried to justify yourself before God and with people instead of firmly standing in your righteousness in Christ?
- Do you have ideas, goals, or practical ways in which you will remind yourself that you have *already* been justified? If you do not make a strategic plan, this wisdom and revelation will not become a reality in your daily life.

DAY TWO

From Death to Life

*For Christ also suffered for sins once for all time, the just for the unjust, so that He might bring us to God, **having been put to death in the flesh, but made alive in the spirit;** in which He also went and made proclamation to the spirits in prison, who once were disobedient when the patience of God kept waiting in the days of Noah, during the construction of the ark, in which a few, that is, eight persons, were brought safely through the water. Corresponding to that, baptism now saves you—not the removal of dirt from the flesh, but an appeal to God for a good conscience—through the resurrection of Jesus Christ, who is at the right hand of God, having gone into heaven, after angels and authorities and powers had been subjected to Him* (1 Peter 3:18–22 NASB).

When you put your faith in Jesus, receiving forgiveness for your sins and salvation, you are *born again.* Some people associate this phrase with a specific Christian denomination or a separate type of religious doctrine, but in John 3:1–17, Jesus explains to Nicodemus, a Pharisee and wise scholar of the Scriptures, how we are first born of the flesh, from our mother's womb, but then through faith in Him, we are born of the Spirit. Thus, being *born again* describes your *spiritual conversion.* Every human being is created with a spirit (and a soul and body). It is why people experience deep spiritual longings, but do not know how to satisfy them until they come into relationship with their Creator.

Although you have a spirit as part of your natural birth, your re-birth spiritually is about coming into a relationship with God through Christ Jesus. This experience should be as memorable as your physical birth. If you cannot remember a specific time when you truly felt the freedom that comes from a relationship with Jesus, I would encourage you to *re-dedicate* your life to Him. Believe and declare the words of the Salvation Prayer found in Appendix 1 at the end of this book, and ask God to reveal Himself to you through His Holy Spirit. The moment you surrender your life to Christ, the Spirit of God will come to live on the inside of you and will partner with your renewed spirit.

When you are born of the Spirit, your old sin nature, which was ruled by the flesh, dies. Your flesh has now been crucified through Christ.

> *I have been crucified with Christ; and it is no longer I who live, but Christ lives in me; and the life which I now live in the flesh I live by faith in the Son of God, who loved me and gave Himself up for me* (Galatians 2:20 NASB).

Being born again means you are now walking in your *full spiritual* identity. Through this experience, you have received a renewed life here on this planet, as well as an eternal life with God, where your spirit will be joined with a glorious and redeemed body. For this present time, we must all wrestle with the battle between our spirit (which has been perfected by the righteousness of Christ) and our flesh, which continues to long for worldly pleasures and is tempted by the enemy to live in sin and shame. The evil realm is constantly trying to talk you out of your God-given destiny and Christ-based identity. To stand firm and live a victorious life, winning as many spiritual battles as possible, you must set your mind on the Kingdom. Seek and pursue a relationship with the Holy Spirit. Meditate on God's Word so as to recognize the Spirit's guidance and direction. This laser-focused mindset is where success and freedom this side of Heaven exist.

> *For those who are in accord with the flesh set their minds on the things of the flesh, but those who are in accord with the Spirit, the things of the Spirit. For the mind set on the flesh is*

> *death, but the mind set on the Spirit is life and peace, because the mind set on the flesh is hostile toward God; for it does not subject itself to the law of God, for it is not even able to do so, and those who are in the flesh cannot please God.… If Christ is in you, though the body is dead because of sin, yet the spirit is alive because of righteousness* (Romans 8:5–8,10 NASB).

So, the question is: Will you choose to die to your flesh, just as Jesus did? Will you take your worldly thoughts, carnal desires, and fleshly longings to the foot of that cross, crucifying them over and over? As you choose to deny your flesh, your spirit will flourish. You will be able to resist temptation and unhealthy, ungodly thinking, and you will live more and more in the victorious freedom of God's truth. This is why living a holy and righteous lifestyle is the will of God for your life. As you choose to be led by the Holy Spirit and deny your worldly desires, you will grow in faith, peace, love, and joy in the Lord. And you will be *exalted*. You will be enabled to fulfill your role in God's Kingdom, magnifying Him and hosting His presence in your life and in the atmosphere around you wherever you go.

Reflection

- Have you heard the term *born-again believer* before? What has it meant to you? What do you believe now (if anything different), and would you say you have experienced a spiritual rebirth?
- Journal or discuss times when you have denied your flesh and what the outcome was. When did you find it most difficult and why? Some issues might be more difficult than others. This is common. We *all* have certain areas of weakness (overeating, abusing alcohol, excessive spending, pornography, jealousy, gossip, etc.).
- Have you spent time with God, reading the Word and following in the steps of an elder or mentor in order to develop intimacy with the Holy Spirit? How have you heard God's voice or felt His presence, direction, or leadership in your life? Have you seen that as you deny your flesh you can feel and hear Him *more*?

DAY THREE

A Tragic Ending

*For Christ also suffered for sins once for all time, the just for the unjust, so that He might bring us to God, having been put to death in the flesh, but made alive in the spirit; in which **He also went and made proclamation to the spirits in prison, who once were disobedient when the patience of God kept waiting in the days of Noah, during the construction of the ark, in which a few, that is, eight persons, were brought safely through the water.** Corresponding to that, baptism now saves you—not the removal of dirt from the flesh, but an appeal to God for a good conscience—through the resurrection of Jesus Christ, who is at the right hand of God, having gone into heaven, after angels and authorities and powers had been subjected to Him* (1 Peter 3:18–22 NASB).

I consider myself a fairly bold person, especially when it comes to sharing my faith, but I also have a people-pleasing nature about me, and I spent many years of my career dancing around some biblical truths so as to not offend those who were unsure of their faith or had no faith at all. But as I continued to strengthen my relationship with the Lord, I eventually felt so convicted by the Holy Spirit that I quit my clinical job and opened my own faith-based practice. This way, I could be free to talk about Jesus as much as I wanted to. As I entered this new practice, in which many of my clients were already Christians (because my business was known for offering spiritual counseling), I was amazed to discover how many of these clients had no knowledge of the *evil spiritual realm* and how much this lack of wisdom affected their daily lives.

Many churches do no specifically teach about Satan and offer little if any training on the types of demonic influence that can exist in a person's life or practical tools for finding spiritual freedom. I have found that it is also rare for churches to spend much time talking about Hell. It is a *real place*, and many, many people are going to spend eternity there. When today's verse says that *Jesus went and proclaimed to the spirits in prison*, it is speaking of the disobedient souls who did not repent when Noah preached to them. They are now awaiting judgment in a spiritual prison that will end in their everlasting suffering in Hell.

Throughout the previous two weeks of Bible study, we have focused on Peter's encouragement to the Church about being steadfast in preaching the Word of God and being a Christ-like example to the world, even in the midst of rejection and persecution. Noah did this for many years, and no one would listen to him. He built a gigantic ark and was ridiculed with disbelief from *everyone* alive at that time. It says that God was patient, and in the King James translation it says He was "longsuffering" toward these people, but in the end, He sent a flood to wipe out the entire world population, except for Noah and his family. Only eight people survived.

So often in the Old Testament, the events that occurred were a foreshadowing of what is to come. The birth, death, and resurrection of Christ was foretold and foreshadowed through hundreds of examples. It was predicted by prophets and reflected in the lives of many *types* of Christ in the holy men of the Old Testament. So is the case with the flood and Noah. Noah did the best He could to preach God's Word and warn the people of their impending death and judgement. This aligns with the prophecies found in the book of Revelation: The percentage of people saved from the flood, *only eight* out of the whole world's population at that time, will be similar to the percentage of people saved in the end times when Jesus returns. Sadly, a very large percentage of this modern world's population will not spend eternity in Heaven, but will experience everlasting suffering in Hell.

Noah was so obedient in building the ark, which was an incredible and impossible feat that could have only happened under the grace and miraculous will of God. If you meditate on this act of faith, you see how incredible Noah's tenacity was for the Lord. In my own times of frustration in praying for breakthrough or having faith for God to answer my prayers, I try to remind myself of Noah's life, as well as the lives of Moses, Joshua, and Joseph. They all suffered faithfully while waiting upon the Lord and trusting in Him to bring all of their efforts and years of not knowing to a glorious completion. This is a good reminder to modern-day holy women (and men) that we must have longsuffering too. It is a fruit of the Spirit given to each believer (see Gal. 5:22) and a Godly attribute. If God can have longsuffering and patience for the disobedient and biblically rebellious, so can we. The example of Noah and the flood should motivate us every day to spread the Good News and to be an example of Jesus to others so that we keep as many souls as possible from being imprisoned for all of eternity.

This heart-breaking reality can be an inspiration for every believer to build their own spiritual ark. This can include businesses, families, ministries, and churches, which might take years of hard labor and relentless effort to build, but they will be safe havens for those in need of a Savior. No matter what the naysayers bring as their defense, as Christ-followers, we must never give up on bringing the truth and hope of Jesus to those in darkness. We must fight to save as many souls as possible from a very real and tragic ending.

Reflection

- How have you made efforts to spread the gospel in your everyday life? God gives grace to all who are obedient. Some will be street evangelists, and others will be homeschool moms raising the next "Billy Graham" of this world. *All positions* of discipling are worthy and valuable in the eyes of the Lord.
- How do the lives of the holy men and women of the Bible inspire you to never give up on speaking the Good News and living your life as an example of who Christ was, for people to witness? In what ways can you be an example for the generations to come?

- Journal or discuss how the fruit of the Spirit of patience or longsuffering is a Godly attribute that you display in your life? With whom? In what kinds of circumstances? Will you have more grace and mercy for difficult people and situations in the future, after today's study?

Jessica Rothmeyer PhD

DAY FOUR

A Life Redeemed

For Christ also suffered for sins once for all time, the just for the unjust, so that He might bring us to God, having been put to death in the flesh, but made alive in the spirit; in which He also went and made proclamation to the spirits in prison, who once were disobedient when the patience of God kept waiting in the days of Noah, during the construction of the ark, in which a few, that is, eight persons, were brought safely through the water. **Corresponding to that, baptism now saves you— not the removal of dirt from the flesh, but an appeal to God for a good conscience—through the resurrection of Jesus Christ,** *who is at the right hand of God, having gone into heaven, after angels and authorities and powers had been subjected to Him* (1 Peter 3:18–22 NASB).

As we discussed yesterday, the Bible is full of symbolism and foreshadowing. As the flood washed the world of sin, so too the act of baptism is a tangible reminder that you have been *washed clean* of sin and death. As you go into the baptizing water, you die to the flesh, and when you re-emerge, you are rising to new life, like Jesus did through the resurrection. You are now redeemed.

The Merriam Webster's 1828 definition of *redeemed* is: "Ransomed; delivered from bondage, distress, penalty, liability, or from the possession of another, by paying an equivalent."[5] The very first word, *ransomed,* makes me

---

5 *Webster's Dictionary:Unabridged,* by Noah Webster, 1828.

think of a movie scenario in which bad guys kidnap an innocent little girl and then ask her parents for a ransom. They have no care or concern for the innocent and precious life of that child; they just want a bunch of money. This is exactly how the evil realm operates. Satan has no regard for human life. Evil spirits are jealous and vengeful toward humans (and each other). Their only desire is to gain power and glory for themselves by keeping humans in bondage. I don't know about you, but whenever I hear of a ransom situation (usually relating to prisoners of war or because of a corrupt government leader), I tend to think, "Don't pay it! They are evil, and if they get away with it, they will just do it again!" Then in my mind, I choose the happy ending in which the good guys find a way to rescue the hostage without giving in to the terrorists. But how does this scenario work out in the Kingdom?

Jesus paid the ransom so that each born-again believer can be set free from bondage, distress, penalty, and liability. His death and resurrection took us from the grips of Satan to the arms of the Father. The possession of ownership transfers *the moment* you accept payment for your sins, which is the blood of Jesus. You have been ransomed by your heavenly Daddy. This demonstrates the powerful definition of being *redeemed*.

If being ransomed—transferred from a prisoner of sin to a citizen of Heaven—was not enough, believers are also washed clean and resurrected through Christ by baptism. A water baptism is a symbol of the washing away of sin and the restoration of Godliness and holiness. But the true miracle is when you are completely overcome by the Spirit of God. Then you know you have been saved, healed, and delivered for a reason and purpose. When you are overcome by the love of the Father and begin to manifest the fruits and gifts of His Spirit, this experience is called being baptized in the Spirit. This might happen at the time of your water baptism or at another significant time. You will realize the purpose of your life is no longer for your own gain or desires, but for the glory and advancement of the Kingdom of God. This revelation will give you a new passion for life. You will never be the same.

> *John responded to them all, saying, "As for me, I baptize you with water; but He is coming who is mightier than I, and I am not fit to untie the straps of His sandals; He will baptize you with the Holy Spirit and fire"* (Luke 3:16 NASB).

The spiritual gift of being filled with the Holy Spirit is often overlooked and misunderstood. Many Christians, while reading their Bibles, will recognize the role of the Holy Spirit in Scripture, but they do not take time to become familiar with and nurture a deep, intimate relationship with Him. God gave us a part of *Himself* to be with us, to literally *do life* with us and bring us passion, fresh revelation, and guidance so we can have victory in the name of Jesus. First, God gave up His Son for 33 years and sacrificed Him as payment for the eternal lives of all humankind. Then, He gave up His Spirit, existing without *this part* of Himself in Heaven until Jesus returns to the earth, when the triune Godhead will be reunited. In James 4:5 it states, *"He jealously desires the Spirit whom He has made to dwell in us."*

Therefore, let us never take for granted the gift of the Holy Spirit, because it is another sacrifice our Father in Heaven made for us because of His amazing love for us and for *our benefit.* The Holy Spirit is jealous of any relationship we have with the world, which disconnects us from Him. He desires more and more of us, but this needs to be a reciprocal relationship. When you are baptized in the Holy Spirit, not only are you cleansed of sin, but you are filled with a supernatural desire for holiness and righteousness. The Holy Spirit cleanses your conscience to be more like God's. But just like any gift, you must open it and use it in order to receive the full advantage of its intended benefits. Just as the resurrection of Christ was the final spiritual step needed to triumph over sin and death, your resurrection *through* Christ declares your own personal victory over any power or bondage the devil throws at you. But you must believe this to be true and walk it out to the *best of your ability.*

Because we are human, our minds and emotions can get the best of us, suffering and life traumas will wear us down, and the chaos and false teachings of this world will distract us, so we need a connection with the Holy Spirit to keep us on track and to intervene in mighty and supernatural ways. He keeps us on that narrow path to holiness and righteousness. We cannot do it alone. God knew that, which is why He sent His Spirit to be with us. I encourage you to nurture an intimate relationship with the Holy Spirit and to continuously use this spiritual gift as the survival tactic it is meant to be in life.

Reflection

- If you have given your life to Jesus, have you been water baptized as an adult? If so, did you experience a tangible washing away of your old worldly life? If you were only baptized as a baby or did not have the *full knowledge* of the spiritual representation of baptism, I would encourage you to meditate on this powerful act of being restored and redeemed. You can even choose to be re-baptized to fully comprehend this powerful spiritual experience.

- Do you make efforts to nurture a relationship with the Holy Spirit? Do you feel His presence and hear His voice? The best way to do this is to approach Him like any other person; talk to Him, spend quality alone time with Him, ask Him questions, and give Him time to respond to you. Learn as much as you can about Him by reading Scripture, so you know how to best relate to Him by understanding His nature.

- If you know someone who seems to have a strong understanding of and visible relationship with the Holy Spirit and who is actively operating in the gifts and fruits of the Spirit, ask that person how they came to that level of intimacy with Him. Have this person pray for you to be baptized with the fire of the Holy Spirit. I am a firm believer in pursing and gleaning wisdom from the elders and mentors that God puts in your life; they are a treasured gift, not to be dismissed or ignored. Those who are already filled with the Spirit are destined to impart an anointing or spiritual mantle to others in order to bring passion and revival to the people of God. In my experience, when a person *earnestly seeks* these gifts, the Holy Spirit is always ready and willing to respond!

DAY FIVE

Seated in Heavenly Places

*For Christ also suffered for sins once for all time, the just for the unjust, so that He might bring us to God, having been put to death in the flesh, but made alive in the spirit; in which He also went and made proclamation to the spirits in prison, who once were disobedient when the patience of God kept waiting in the days of Noah, during the construction of the ark, in which a few, that is, eight persons, were brought safely through the water. Corresponding to that, baptism now saves you—not the removal of dirt from the flesh, but an appeal to God for a good conscience—through the resurrection of Jesus Christ, **who is at the right hand of God, having gone into heaven, after angels and authorities and powers had been subjected to Him** (1 Peter 3:18–22 NASB).*

In the latter section of yesterday's study, we established that Jesus' resurrection from the dead was the ultimate triumph in the spiritual realm. Satan celebrated a little too early when Jesus was crucified. In reality, the enemy was about to be defeated. Three days later, when Jesus overcame death and broke the curse of Adam, He became the Savior for all humankind. When today's verse mentions *"authorities and powers,"* it is referring to the evil realm. When Jesus took His place at the right hand of the Father in Heaven, all angels, authorities, and powers were subjected in total submission to Him.

It was some time into my spiritual journey before I heard a sermon that pointed out the significance of this phrase (which is located in multiple places in the Bible): *"Jesus was seated."* These words were not written in a willy-nilly fashion; they indicate that Jesus is now at rest. He finished what He came to do. The fact that He is *seated* in Heaven, next to His Father, signifies that His authority and spiritual power have come to full completion. He had conquered it all (sin, death, evil forces), and now the spiritual law is fulfilled. Nothing was left for Jesus to do, so He *sat* down.

> *I pray that the eyes of your heart may be enlightened, so that you will know what is the hope of His calling, what are the riches of the glory of His inheritance in the saints, and what is the boundless greatness of His power toward us who believe. These are in accordance with the working of the strength of His might which He brought about in Christ, when He raised Him from the dead and seated Him at His right hand in the heavenly places, far above all rule and authority and power and dominion, and every name that is named, not only in this age but also in the one to come* (Ephesians 1:18–21 NASB).

Jesus will continue to rest in His position of power and authority, next to His Heavenly Father, until the day He returns, the final judgment, when He will establish peace and righteousness and reign on the earth. If this future destiny for believers is not thrilling enough, Scripture says we *share* in this same spiritual power and authority through Christ Jesus, not just someday, but *now.*

> *But God, being rich in mercy, because of His great love with which He loved us, even when we were dead in our wrongdoings, made us alive together with Christ (by grace you have been saved), and raised us up with Him, and seated us with Him in the heavenly places in Christ Jesus* (Ephesians 2:4–6 NASB).

So, not only have we been forgiven, adopted into the Holy Family, and given the gift of eternal life, but we also have received from God, because of His rich mercy and love, the ability to share in the power and authority given to Christ. We have been raised up with Him and He *seated us* with Christ in heavenly places. Today. Not when you die and go to Heaven, but *today*. The moment you are born again, experiencing your spiritual conversion, you receive dual citizenship. You are no longer just flesh and blood, but you are also a heavenly creature, seated in heavenly places with all of the angels, authorities, and powers subjected and in submission to *you*. You are *seated* just like Jesus, because you bear the full identity of His righteousness in you!

Can you imagine just how powerful modern-day women (and the whole Body of Christ) could be if we exercised our *full* spiritual authority? We could change the lives of many people, making the name of Jesus known throughout the world. And then, all the efforts of the enemy to disrupt, distract, and destroy our lives would be futile and lose traction. Satan would gain no return on his investments in trying to steal our joy and cause chaos in our lives. Who does he think he is anyway? He is beneath our feet!

> *Behold, I have given you authority to walk on snakes and scorpions, and authority over all the power of the enemy, and nothing will injure you. Nevertheless, do not rejoice in this, that the spirits are subject to you, but rejoice that your names are recorded in heaven* (Luke 10:19–20 NASB).

Satan and his evil army are already defeated, and he knows it. Like the unjust and evil prince that he is, he is now trying to cause as much trouble as possible before believers figure out his game. When Jesus returns, Satan will be bound from having any ability to affect the lives of God's people, ever again.

Reflection

- Did you realize, before today's study, that you were already seated in heavenly places? If so, how have you exercised your authority in the spiritual realm against Satan and his evil army? Have you done it through prayer, declarations, decrees, teaching, or training others in the Word?

- If not, how will this change your outlook, thinking, choices, and influence in the world as you walk in righteousness, power, and authority as a modern-day holy woman?

Jessica Rothmeyer PhD

EPILOGUE

There is a battle for your soul. Satan wants to steal, strip, and hide your Kingdom assignment. Learning to have the mind of Christ and walk in the holiness and righteousness you *already have* is a life-changing principle that will enable you to walk in your God-given identity. Being a modern-day holy woman is about learning to think like God thinks about life, pain, and love. Applying these Kingdom principles to your life will produce healing and freedom like you have never imagined. I encourage you to read and re-read this book, and *study* (not just read) your Bible every day. I urge you to find a network of like-minded Christian women. We all need a tribe to hold us up when we are tired and keep us on the narrow-yet-glorious path to a holy and God-honoring lifestyle. This *is* the heartbeat of God; He cherishes His daughters, and He has a very significant calling on your life. Your Kingdom destiny awaits.

APPENDICES: PRAYERS AND BIBLE VERSES

APPENDIX 1

Salvation Prayer

(Your Spiritual Birth)

The path to salvation is to declare aloud and believe in your heart that Jesus is your Savior. First, *believe* He died for your sins, and second, *receive* the forgiveness that is necessary for you to spend eternal life in Heaven with God. This surrender is the most important step you can make in your lifetime. Life *is* eternal; every human being must make a choice about where they will spend their eternity. If you would like to experience your spiritual birth today, pray this prayer aloud and *believe* the words to be true as you declare them:

> *Heavenly Father, I know I am a sinner, and I need forgiveness. I confess right now that Jesus died on the cross for me. He shed His blood as payment for my sins, past, current, and future. I accept the gift of forgiveness and choose to make Jesus the Lord and leader of my life. I accept the gift of eternal life with You, Father God, in Heaven someday. I invite the Holy Spirit to fill me. Show me all that You are Lord and how to follow You. I give You my life. In Jesus' name I pray. Amen.*

APPENDIX 2

Your Identity in Christ

I am complete in Jesus, who is the head over all rule and authority—over every angelic and earthly power (see Col. 2:10).

I am alive with Christ (see Eph. 2:5).

I am free from the law of sin and death (see Rom. 8:2).

I am far from oppression and will not live in fear (see Isa. 54:14).

I am born of God, and the evil one does not touch me (see 1 John 5:18).

I am holy and without blame before Him in love (see Eph.1:4; 1 Pet. 1:16).

I have the mind of Christ (see 1 Cor. 2:16; Phil. 2:5).

I have the peace of God that surpasses all understanding (see Phil. 4:7).

The Spirit of God, who is greater than the enemy in the world, lives in me (see 1 John 4:4).

I have received abundant grace and the gift of righteousness, and I reign in life through Jesus Christ (see Rom. 5:17).

I have received the Spirit of wisdom and revelation in the knowledge of Jesus, the eyes of my heart being enlightened, so that I know the hope of having life in Christ (see Eph. 1:17–18).

I have received the power of the Holy Spirit, and He can do miraculous things through me. I have authority and power over the enemy in this world (see Mark 16:17–18; Luke 10:17–19).

I am renewed in the knowledge of God and no longer want to live in my old ways or nature before I accepted Christ (see Col. 3:9–10).

I am merciful, I do not judge others, and I forgive quickly. As I do this by God's grace, He blesses my life (see Luke 6:36–38).

God supplies all of my needs according to His riches in glory in Christ Jesus (see Phil. 4:19).

In all circumstances, I live by faith in God and extinguish all the flaming darts (attacks) of the enemy (see Eph. 6:16).

I can do whatever I need to do in life through Christ Jesus who gives me strength (see Phil. 4:13).

I am chosen by God, who called me out of the darkness of sin and into the light and life of Christ so I can proclaim the excellence and greatness of who He is (see 1 Pet. 2:9).

I am born again—spiritually transformed, renewed, and set apart for God's purpose—through the living and everlasting word of God (see 1 Pet. 1:23).

I am God's workmanship, created in Christ to do good works that He has prepared for me to do (see Eph. 2:10).

I am a new creation in Christ (see 2 Cor. 5:17).

In Christ, I am dead to sin—my relationship to it is broken—and alive to God—living in unbroken fellowship with Him (see Rom. 6:11).

The light of God's truth shines in my heart and gives me knowledge of salvation through Christ (see 2 Cor. 4:6).

As I hear God's Word, I do what it says and am blessed in my actions (see James 1:22, 25).

I am a joint-heir with Christ (see Rom. 8:17).

I am more than a conqueror through Him who loves me (see Rom. 8:37).

I overcome the enemy of my soul by the blood of the Lamb and the word of my testimony (see Rev. 12:11).

I have everything I need to live a godly life, and I am equipped to live in His divine nature (see 2 Pet. 1:3–4).

I am an ambassador for Christ (see 2 Cor. 5:20).

I am part of a chosen generation, a royal priesthood, a holy nation, a purchased people (see 1 Pet. 2:9).

I am the righteousness of God—I have right standing with Him—in Jesus Christ (see 2 Cor. 5:21).

My body is a temple of the Holy Spirit; I belong to Him (see 1 Cor. 6:19).

I am the head and not the tail, and I only go up and not down in life as I trust and obey God (see Deut. 28:13).

I am chosen by God, forgiven, and justified through Christ. I have a compassionate heart, kindness, humility, meekness, and patience (see Rom. 8:33; Col. 3:12).

I am redeemed—forgiven of all my sins and made clean—through the blood of Christ (see Eph. 1:7).

I have been rescued from the domain and power of darkness and brought into God's Kingdom (see Col. 1:13).

I am redeemed from the curse of sin, sickness, and poverty (see Deut. 28:15–68; Gal. 3:13).

My life is rooted in my faith in Christ, and I overflow with thanksgiving for all He has done for me (see Col. 2:7).

I am called to live a holy life by the grace of God and to declare His praise in the world (see Ps. 66:8; 2 Tim. 1:9).

I am healed and whole in Jesus (see Isa. 53:5; 1 Pet. 2:24).

I am saved by God's grace, raised up with Christ, and seated with Him in heavenly places (see Eph. 2:5–6; Col. 2:12).

I am greatly loved by God (see John 3:16; Eph. 2:4; Col. 3:12; 1 Thess. 1:4).

I am strengthened with all power according to His glorious might (see Col. 1:11).

I humbly submit myself to God, and the devil flees from me because I resist him in the name of Jesus (see James 4:7).

I press on each day to fulfill God's plan for my life because I live to please Him (see Phil. 3:14).

I am not ruled by fear because the Holy Spirit lives in me and gives me His power, love, and self-control (see 2 Tim. 1:7).

Christ lives in me, and I live by faith in Him and His love for me (see Gal. 2:20).

APPENDIX 3

Prayer to Break the Curse of a Diagnosis

Doctors, teachers, psychologists, friends, and family can intentionally or inadvertently speak the curse of a diagnosis against you and onto your life. If you begin to agree with these suggestions, observations, or verdicts, then you give Satan dominion to manifest those symptoms even more in your life. It will be difficult to receive supernatural healing from God without taking the critical step of breaking the curse *and* any agreements you have made with the "world". The following prayer is an example; please feel free to make it personal and add more as you feel led by the Holy Spirit.

> *Heavenly Father, I come before You and repent for believing Satan's lies, the false knowledge/worldly authorities who spoke nthat I have _____(name diagnosis). I apply the blood of Jesus to my sin of believing these lies, and I break the curse of _____ that was spoken against me in Jesus' mighty name. I rebuke the agreement I made in admitting to, claiming, and/or trying to medically treat _____ in Jesus' name. I break any partnership I have made with an authority in this world, I stand with You, Father God, as my Creator, Physician and the one true Authority in my life. I align my mind, will emotions with the Spirit of truth, the Holy Spirit within me. I apply the blood of Jesus to all of my family lines that have also believed and accepted the curse of _____. I stand in agreement with the Word of God that Jesus died for all sins*

and iniquities, and I declare that I am saved, healed, and delivered by His blood. I have been made excellent of soul by the power of His resurrection. I declare these Scriptures over my life to reaffirm my commitment to You, Lord Jesus, and all that You sacrificed for me so that I can walk in divine health, to live a life more abundant!

Continue by declaring the following verses and ending with the prayer at the bottom of this page.

But He was pierced for our offenses, He was crushed for our wrongdoings; the punishment for our well-being was laid upon Him, and by His wounds we are healed (Isaiah 53:5 NASB).

Therefore, if anyone is in Christ, this person is a new creation; the old things passed away; behold, new things have come (2 Corinthians 5:17 NASB).

For God has not given us a spirit of timidity, but of power [resurrection power/miracle healing power] *and love and discipline* (2 Timothy 1:7 NASB).

And He has said to me, "My grace is sufficient for you, for power is perfected in weakness." Most gladly, therefore, I will rather boast about my weaknesses, so that the power of Christ may dwell in me (2 Corinthians 12:9 NASB).

For you created my innermost parts [my mind]; *You wove me in my mother's womb. I will give thanks to You, because I am awesomely and wonderfully made; wonderful are your works, and my soul knows it very well* (Psalm 139:13–14 NASB).

And not only this, but we also celebrate in our tribulations, knowing that tribulation brings about perseverance; and perseverance, proven character; and proven character, hope; and hope does not disappoint, because the love of God has been poured out within our hearts through the Holy Spirit who was given to us (Romans 5:3–5 NASB).

I receive forgiveness from You today, Lord, and I forgive all who have spoken curses over me, my healthy or my family. I pray they receive wisdom about Your truth, Father God. I ask You to use the Holy Spirit within me to guide me in the times I struggle with familiar symptoms and to remind me of my agreement with You, Your Word and Your Kingdom only. I declare today that I walk in the divine health that the blood of Jesus bought for me. In the redemptive and restorative name of Jesus I pray. Amen.

APPENDIX 4

Joy in Suffering

Consider it all joy, my brothers and sisters, when you encounter various trials, knowing that the testing of your faith produces endurance. And let endurance have its perfect result, so that you may be perfect and complete, lacking in nothing (James 1:2–4).

And not only this, but we also celebrate in our tribulations, knowing that tribulation brings about perseverance; and perseverance, proven character; and proven character, hope; and hope does not disappoint, because the love of God has been poured out within our hearts through the Holy Spirit who was given to us (Romans 5:3–5).

Therefore I delight in weaknesses, in insults, in distresses, in persecutions, in difficulties, in behalf of Christ; for when I am weak, then I am strong (2 Corinthians 12:10).

Be devoted to one another in brotherly love; give preference to one another in honor, not lagging behind in diligence, fervent in spirit, serving the Lord; rejoicing in hope, persevering in tribulation, devoted to prayer (Romans 12:10–12).

For I consider that the sufferings of this present time are not worthy to be compared with the glory that is to be revealed to us (Romans 8:18).

Now I rejoice in my sufferings for your sake, and in my flesh I am supplementing what is lacking in Christ's afflictions in behalf of His body, which is the church (Colossians 1:24).

And we know that God causes all things to work together for good to those who love God, to those who are called according to His purpose (Romans 8:28).

For His anger is but for a moment, His favor is for a lifetime; weeping may last for the night, but a shout of joy comes in the morning (Psalm 30:5).

For the moment, all discipline seems not to be pleasant, but painful; yet to those who have been trained by it, afterward it yields the peaceful fruit of righteousness (Hebrews 12:11).

Blessed be the God and Father of our Lord Jesus Christ, the Father of mercies and God of all comfort, who comforts us in all our affliction so that we will be able to comfort those who are in any affliction with the comfort with which we ourselves are comforted by God (2 Corinthians 1:3–4).

After you have suffered for a little while, the God of all grace, who called you to His eternal glory in Christ, will Himself perfect, confirm, strengthen, and establish you (1 Peter 5:10).

For our momentary, light affliction is producing for us an eternal weight of glory far beyond all comparison (2 Corinthians 4:17).

That I may know Him and the power of His resurrection and the fellowship of His sufferings, being conformed to His death (Philippians 3:10).

So they went on their way from the presence of the Council, rejoicing that they had been considered worthy to suffer shame for His name (Acts 5:41).

For to you it has been granted for Christ's sake, not only to believe in Him, but also to suffer on His behalf (Philippians 1:29).

Who will separate us from the love of Christ? Will tribulation, or trouble, or persecution, or famine, or nakedness, or danger, or sword? (Romans 8:35).

The afflictions of the righteous are many, but the Lord rescues him from them all (Psalm 34:19).

For you have been called for this purpose, because Christ also suffered for you, leaving you an example, so that you would follow in His steps (1 Peter 2:21).

And if children, heirs also, heirs of God and fellow heirs with Christ, if indeed we suffer with Him so that we may also be glorified with Him (Romans 8:17).

Rejoice and be glad, for your reward in heaven is great; for in this same way they persecuted the prophets who were before you (Matthew 5:12).

Beloved, do not be surprised at the fiery ordeal among you, which comes upon you for your testing, as though something strange were happening to you; but to the degree that you share the sufferings of Christ, keep on rejoicing, so that at the revelation of His glory you may also rejoice and be overjoyed (1 Peter 4:12–13).

Blessed is a man who perseveres under trial; for once he has been approved, he will receive the crown of life which the Lord has promised to those who love Him (James 1:12).

Blessed are those who have been persecuted for the sake of righteousness, for theirs is the kingdom of heaven. Blessed are you when people insult you and persecute you, and falsely say all kinds of evil against you because of Me. Rejoice and be glad, for your reward in heaven is great; for in this same way they persecuted the prophets who were before you (Matthew 5:10–12).

Do not fear what you are about to suffer. Behold, the devil is about to throw some of you into prison, so that you will be tested, and you will have tribulation for ten days. Be faithful until death, and I will give you the crown of life (Revelation 2:10).

These things I have spoken to you so that in Me you may have peace. In the world you have tribulation but take courage; I have overcome the world (John 16:33).

Printed in the United States
by Baker & Taylor Publisher Services